# BLOOD ON THE TRACKS

## THE STORY OF BOB DYLAN

# BLOOD ON THE TRACKS

## THE STORY OF
# BOB DYLAN

## Chris Rowley

**PROTEUS BOOKS**
LONDON/NEW YORK

PROTEUS BOOKS is an imprint of
The Proteus Publishing Group

*United States*
PROTEUS PUBLISHING CO., INC.
9 West 57th Street, Suite 4503
New York, NY 10019
*distributed by:*
CHERRY LANE BOOKS CO., INC.
PO Box 430,
Port Chester, NY 10573

*United Kingdom*
PROTEUS BOOKS LIMITED
Bremar House,
Sale Place,
London W2 1PT

ISBN 0 86276 127 1 (p/b)
0 86276 128 X (h/b)

First published in US 1984
First published in UK 1984

*Photocredits:*
Cyrus Andrews, Aquarius Literary Agency, Keystone Press Agency
Fred McDarrah, Michael Petrello, Paul Natkin
*Photo Reserve:*
Barry Plummer, David Redfern, Rex Features, Howard Rosenberg,
Joseph Sia, Frank Spooner Pictures, Star File

*Editor:* Kay Rowley
*Designed by:* Adrian Hodgkins
*Typeset by:* Wordsmith Limited
*Printed* in Great Britain by
Chanctonbury Press

# CHAPTER ONE

# Little Minnesota Town

'You can stand at one end of Hibbing on the main drag and see
clear past the city limits on the other end.'
Bob Dylan *My Life In A Stolen Moment* 1963.

As a young man not yet out of his teens, Bob Dylan came
out of – what was for him – the cultural equivalent of a
howling wilderness. He had a fire lit in his imagination and a
dream that trembled inside him. It was vague still, as he had
little real idea of how to control it yet, but already he knew
what it was he wanted and the intensity with which he wanted
it impressed itself on many of those who knew him at the time.
He felt a primal urge to seize hold of an audience, to grip
people's attention and hold them spellbound with song. He
was determined to be a performer, and a successful one. To
this end he felt his whole life had been turned and shaped.
There was simply nothing else to do.

Indeed, failure was something he couldn't allow himself to
contemplate from a very early point, maybe even by the time
he was fifteen or sixteen, Robert Zimmerman had felt the call
of the dream, the urge to "make it", to follow in the footsteps
of idols like Hank Williams, even Elvis Presley, and surface
from the depths of the ocean of American dreams to occupy
the heights.

It was the only way out, for he was seeking not just a route
out of the little Minnesota town he grew up in, but also a way
free from the claustrophobically uptight culture of the fifties.
To escape once was not enough; anyone could ride down
Highway 61 to Minneapolis and see the world outside Hibbing,
but only the gifted and determined few could lift themselves
free from the clutch of American culture, from the dreams and
the hatreds and the shattering tedium.

Like so many thousands of other young men and women
burning with a similar desire to escape from humdrum
surroundings and a chance to affect the world around them,
he plotted his escape. Since success would depend on his
abilities as a songster and guitar strummin' gypsy, he re-

searched the field of popular music with great thoroughness. As it turned out, he was an excellent student of the musical forms that were later to coalesce in the sixties to form Rock Music.

Of course his ambitions were outrageously romantic and a source of sorrow to his father, nor was it a case of his having to make it to escape the grind of poverty. His father, Abe Zimmerman, was doing just fine in his business under the wash of prosperity that characterized the great boom in the American economy from the late forties to the end of the sixties. The dream burned in his brain however. In his second year of High School he told his closest friends Echo Helstrom and John Buckland that he needed a new name, a stage persona, and then something more. He had made a definite commitment to himself to become a successful musical performer.

Naturally, his father dreaded that dream and fought to subdue it in his eldest son. Abe Zimmerman had known an earlier America, one that by the fifties lived on only in the memories of those who'd survived the Depression. Abe knew that hard times were really *hard* and he could easily envisage the despair that failure could produce in young Robert's chosen field, nor could he picture Rock 'n' Roll as a real career choice; it went entirely against the grain of the Zimmerman family.

Partly as a result of that parental pressure to conform, to give up the dream and settle down to running the family hardware store, Bob Dylan's first incarnation on the world stage was that of an orphan. Someone who'd never wanted to be from anywhere in particular anyway. Someone who was certifiably heading for someplace, though except that he wasn't entirely sure just where it might be.

One thing Robert Alan Zimmerman most certainly wasn't was one who would graduate from Hibbing High and go to college and learn accountancy and go back to the iron range and work in his father's store. That persona was never allowed out the door, it was smothered and buried in a closet and left behind in Hibbing. Instead, Bob Dylan came on like Ariel, on the winds, as a breath of the grand old struggle, a whiff of dust and sweat just barely held together by joy, up from Oklahoma on a freight train via the Turpentine Work Camps and, most important of all, from those "Dusty Old Fairgrounds" where the circus boys, linament salesmen and the folksingers played.

Thus, in his initial onslaught on an unsuspecting world, the young Dylan explained that he had no parents. He didn't come from anywhere precisely except from the whole wide Mid-West.

If any particular locus of origin was demanded, then he would own to being an Okie kid, born travelling those dusty roads. His home life as a child was insignificant. He'd been running away since he was ten. Every year he'd have a guitar and harmonica in hand, seeking the travelling shows and the carnivals and the folksingers. Every year he'd get caught after a while, sent home and whopped a bit to make him settle down. Of course, it never worked – in the end he escaped.

This was the fantasy. In fact Dylan came from an ordinary, very nice Jewish-American family – not wealthy, but not poor by any means. It is highly unlikely that he ever set foot in Oklahoma.

His people had originally come to the north country of Wisconsin around the turn of the century from Odessa, in Russia. His mother's family settled initially in Superior, a logging center, then moved on. They were in the theatre business. They moved up to Hibbing, Minnesota on the Mesabi Iron Range where they ran a clothing store while another branch of the family, the Edelsteins, operated the Lybba Movie Theatre, continuing the family theatrical tradition. The Zimmermans were established in Duluth, just across from Superior, Wisconsin, where they owned a shoe store.

Robert Alan Zimmerman was born in Duluth on May 24th 1941, and spent his first six years there. Shortly after his brother David was born in 1947, the family moved to Hibbing (his mother Beattie's home town). Abe Zimmerman became a partner in Micka Electric, a hardware, electric supply and appliance store on Fifth Avenue, just off Howard Street, Hibbing's main drag.

At first, they rented an apartment but soon Abe was able to buy a house, a rectangular flat top, sheated in stucco on Seventh Ave. Times were good. Americans were buying great quantities of electric consumer goods. The national GNP was in the throes of doubling every five years.

Robert was a bright but shy kid. In his mother's words, he was a "doer and goer" who "particularly enjoyed playing basketball." But he was to recall later that "he never had friends back then" in the fourth grade, and that he was essentially a loner. His interests lay elsewhere. He was teaching himself to play the piano, and he wrote poems.

'I don't know if most people write when they're eight or nine you know, but I actually did write poems at that age. Poems that rhymed, you know, for the flowers and my mother and stuff like that...', he told an interviewer years later.

9

A sensitive kid clearly, and one that continued to branch out musically. He soon included the harmonica in his repertoire and since his dad was paying him to work on his truck and help with deliveries, young Robert soon achieved his next objective:

> I saved the money I had made working on my Daddy's
> truck and bought a Silvertone guitar from Sears Roebuck.
> I was twelve. I just bought a book of chords and began to
> play. The first song I wrote was a song to Brigitte Bardot.'

Piano, harmonica, guitar and poems to his mother and Brigitte Bardot by the time he was thirteen, Bobby Zimmerman had all the equipment on his hands that he was ever going to need.

Furthermore, although he might justifiably claim to have been born in the wrong place, Hibbing *was* virtually on the edge of nowhere – he'd certainly been born into interesting times. He was to grow up on a culture curve that exposed him to all the key elements of Rock and Folk and even superstardom in perfect sequence.

Nineteen forty-one itself was a vital year. A cusp between the old pre-War America, mired in desperate economic depression for a decade, and the new America that was to revolutionize the World in a few short years. With war orders pouring in, the economy had at last begun to move. Entry into the war itself brought on a tide of growth. Of course it was also a desperate year for lovers of freedom, as the forces of Nazi Germany and Japan were on the ascendant. The shock of the war, however, served to finally shatter the old Eurocentric world and usher in the modern age. Young Robert Zimmerman was, of course, largely unaware of the great events going on, just as he was unaware of the smaller turns of fate that were shaping the new world.

For example, just a few years before, in 1938, the electric guitar had made its appearance in the world of jazz and black blues music. Charlie Christian of the Benny Goodman Band was using the electric guitar, but in the virtuoso high speed runs and note clusters that acoustic jazz guitarists had used before.

Elsewhere, T-Bone Walker, a Texas blues singer, variated it in a new way, using distortion and twists of amplifier control to extend notes and alter pitch, while combining these new tricks with all the old ones familiar to acoustic guitarists for years.

Another prime example had actually taken place the year

10

before. In 1940, Alan Lomax got Woody Guthrie to sit down long enough to record the historic Library of Congress recordings, capturing forever the tales and songs of the Okies on the roads and rails.

An even more important event for Robert Zimmerman's future was the rift, also in 1940, between the American Society of Composers, Authors and Publishers (ASCAP) and broadcast radio. This lead to the start of Broadcast Music Incorporated as a new channel of licensing recorded music to be played on radio. Since ASCAP had never favored music by blacks or hillbillies, it opened up radio to such proletarian forms as never before. From the start, BMI had a virtual monopoly on this music. ASCAP had previously dominated music sales and radio, while ASCAP and Tin Pan Alley, with the sophisticated sound of New York and Hollywood, were hand in hand.

With Broadway, Hollywood and Tin Pan Alley on its side, ASCAP seemed invincible, except that the tide of history and technology was turning in the direction of recorded music radio formats. BMI soon prospered, along with small radio stations and small independent radio networks outside the pull of the Tin Pan Alley-dominated majors. This gave the small independent labels their big chance and by the end of the forties, Atlantic Records, King, Savoy, Imperial, Aladdin and many others were driving a wedge into the near monopoly that the majors like Columbia, RCA and Decca had previously enjoyed as far as national distribution was concerned. Local radio stations were creating new regional markets for records. A host of new performers, with stronger, earthier music than anything from New York, were suddenly finding outlets and recording contracts. From Hank Williams to Muddy Waters, the phenomenon spread across the Mid-West, the heartland of America. Soon the mainstream pop charts were joined by the country & western and rhythm 'n' blues charts as gauges of popular music. Once again, proletarian culture occupied a sector dominated by elite tastes.

Other factors were also at work, altering forever the fabric of American life. Television became increasingly important during the forties, and in the fifties it brought about a revolution in tastes and habits.

For example, the patterns of beer consumption by Americans (99% Male) changed drastically in step with television. Canned beer had first made an appearance in '35 as a novelty, although it was the butt of a million jokes. Beer was still something men drank in bars and taprooms and occasionally from a bottle at

11

home. Local breweries and regional beers were the rule. During the early fifties, beer consumption shifted rapidly to home consumption. Women now became the major purchasers and they bought their husbands' beer in the supermarkets where price, display and packaging counted for everything. The new national brands like Schlitz and Budweiser took off at a gallop and the influence of bars and taprooms shrank to insignificance.

This was also a time of great social conflict and international paranoia. The Cold War was at its height. The new menace of the A-bomb was joined by its bigger cousin the H-bomb and the world lived with the new concept of total self-annihilation. Robert Zimmerman was fortunate enough to be too young for the Korean War, as later he was too old for the Vietnam War, but nobody could escape the effects of the Cold War and the rise of the American Right.

The trials of the Rosenbergs on charges of selling nuclear weapons secrets to the Russians, and the trial of Alger Hiss had helped to create the sense of frenzy. Richard Nixon became Vice-President and the House Un-American Activities Committee was pursuing its witch-hunt against communists and suspected communists in the entertainment industry. Informers and stool pigeons sprang out of the woodwork to turn in their former friends and idealistic acquaintances. In the Senate, Joe McCarthy rose to prominence as his Senate Permanent Subcommittee on Investigations went after noted liberals and critics of the witch-hunts.

Abroad in the land, the American Legion, two million eight hundred thousand strong, was busy searching out "subversives" and denouncing them to the FBI. The FBI was in the active business of ruining the careers of anyone who had ever had dealings with the Left. A whisper here lost someone his job, a whisper there ensured he or she would never be hired again. The American Communist Party which, even at its height during the alliance with Russia during World War II, had never boasted more than seventy-five thousand members, was routed and virtually destroyed. But this was only one effect; in Hollywood, in publishing, in virtually every walk of life, the threat of informers and the blacklist pushed dissenting voices into the dark.

Finally there was the strange fact of racial segregation, a weird poison from the past that was working away in the nation's blood. In World War II, the American armed services that fought Hitler and Japan were racially segregated. In the fifties black men were still being convicted and executed on paltry evidence for a variety of non-lethal crimes. Lynchings and mob-killings in the southern states were not unknown.

The workings of official racism were oddly pathological. Not until 1943 for instance, was a black man ever to kiss a white woman on the Broadway stage. Then Paul Robeson, in *Othello*, did it and went on to set a Broadway record for performances of a Shakespeare play, eventually appearing two hundred and ninety-five times. A few years later though, Robeson was being denounced as an enemy of America. In 1950 his passport was revoked and he was unable to travel abroad to continue his work of calling attention to the plight of the downtrodden black minority in the USA.

Denying an American citizen a passport, even the whole crazy quilt of paranoia involved in HUAC and McCarthyism, seems faintly incredible today, but in Robert Zimmerman's childhood these events were shaping headlines and TV news just as much as the wars and the H-bomb.

The fifties were for America a time of inordinate family growth resulting in a wave of children – the great 'baby boom' – coupled with a swift rise in suburban living produced, among other effects, a tidal wave of paranoia. In addition to the Russians and the Bomb, the great scares of the time were Polio, the virus of paralysis, and flying saucers. On several occasions the saucers made headlines and the Air Force was even driven to open a series of investigations into UFOs, just to appease a public uneasy at the thought of alienated objects flying through American skies.

Meanwhile, every few months, the TVs of the nation lit up with the stark image of another hydrogen bomb test.

But if nuclear technology ruled the headlines and the news, other forms of technological advance were continuing unabated. In 1948, Columbia introduced the 33 & ½ rpm long playing disc. Entire Broadway shows such as *Oklahoma* and *South Pacific* could be released on one or two records instead of a box of 78s. Long pieces of music could be played without the constant annoyance of changing the records. Sales of records took off in the late forties and kept climbing steadily. In 1945, the record companies had been doing ninety million dollars worth of business; by 1950, they had topped the two hundred million mark.

However, the popular music charts were still dominated by the major companies and by the bland mainstream pop music they preferred to market.

Robert Zimmerman soon found that the most interesting

place in town for him was Crippa's, the only record store. It was there during eighth grade, when he was not quite fourteen, that he came across the records of Hank Williams. Compared to the majority of pop tunes, Williams' songs were tangy and strong, exhilarating, forceful music. Years later, Dylan described Williams as his first idol.

Of course, Williams was already dead (January 1, 1953 in a car accident) but his importance for Bob Dylan's career should not be underestimated. Talking about his own initial impetus towards singing, a young Dylan in 1961 commented:

I just did it you know. I started singing after I started writing. I started that when I was ten or eleven, and started out country & western, Hank Williams and Lefty Frizell kinda things. Hank Williams had just died and I started playing sometime around there.

'Hank Williams was the first influence I would think. I guess for a longer period of time than anybody else influenced me.

Bob bought all the Hank Williams records that Crippa's had on hand and ordered the rest. His interest in authentic-sounding popular music had truly begun.

He began to comb the airwaves on the family radio, moving away from the networks. At night he could pick up signals from black stations far away to the south. From down in Arkansas, in the rhythm 'n' blues belt, he picked up on the program of Gatemouth Page. He may even have heard the Poppa Stoppa in New Orleans and Alan Freed's show in Cleveland. These were white stations that were starting to introduce black rock 'n' roll music to white teenage audiences. Very likely he heard the shows of Wolfman Jack broadcast by a super-powerful pirate station on the border with Mexico. The station's power was enormous and on clear nights the Wolfman was heard right across the Mid-West, clear to the Canadian border.

Nineteen fifty-five was a magical year, a year of great transformation, births and deaths. A watershed year, a crucial turning point for Robert Zimmerman and for millions of others. The economic boom continued to raise all boats on the tide of American consumerism and now bubbling beneath the surface of the culture were strong new forms of expression.

The Method Acting School had unloosed powerful new talents for screen and stage including Marlon Brando and James Dean. Dean was to be the first great male media God, forever untarnished thanks to an early death.

Dean, Brando and Marilyn Monroe were all exposing

Americans to a new kind of rebellion, and a wholly new level of sensual revelation.

It was also the year of TV. Sets were so common now that TV had a society-wide market. Watching television had become the predominant evening leisure activity for adult Americans. As a direct consequence, television was extremely "square" and pretty boring. Programming was designed not to give offence to puritanical older generations, which didn't connect for teens who sought release from the tensions of the times.

The answer to this need for specifically young styled forms of expression was already being cut in small recording studios, like that of Sun Records in Memphis, Tennessee, where Elvis Presley had cut *That's Alright Mama* and his other country & western chart hits.

Rising like sap through layers of restriction and social pressures, the heavy, intrinsically danceable rhythms of black rock 'n' roll were breaking into white popular music. From 1950 onwards, boogie-woogie had been popular in both black Rhythm 'n' Blues and some kinds of Country & Western. Electric guitar had percolated from Memphis to Nashville, giving hard edges and a searing tone to the new music.

At the end of 1954, Link Wray had a huge hit with an instrumental rocker (*Rumble*) that perfectly expressed the state of the art of hillbilly black crossover. It was electric guitar rock, the first example of what is now known as heavy metal music.

The record charts began to reflect the generation gap that was appearing. The split could be charted by the acceptance of black musical forms with a heavy beat. "Jungle music", snarled middle-aged critics. The kids responded by going to the hop.

Elsewhere, another kind of rebellion, that of the intellectually hip and alienated, was stirring new waves. Jack Kerouac had written and published *On The Road* and the Beat Generation was bopping to the music of Charlie Parker and the be-bop jazzmen while espousing marijuana, zen, wine and poetry in a confusing, if exciting *mélange*. Allen Ginsberg had shaken the marbled sublimity of American poetry criticism with his output beginning with *Howl* and with the Conservative Right in such absolute control of cultural forms of expression, there were soon hundreds of beats or beatniks on the road. The Beat Generation raised the banner of intellectual rebellion to the alienating effects of the new industrial age. Coffee shops and poetry magazines sprouted on campuses across the nation. Zen, folk music and copies of *On The Road* were suddenly essential for a certain type of college student.

If American political, academic and cultural institutions were in the grip of reactionaries and red-baiters, the culture beyond institutional control was not, and down there things were shaking loose.

Bob Zimmerman saw James Dean's best films, *East Of Eden* and *Rebel Without A Cause* that year, and thus was caught up with the rest of his generation in the sorrow of Dean's death, resulting from a tragic auto accident on the road to Salinas, California. Friends of his from that time have recalled that Bob was a definite Dean fan who bought up magazines that had any articles on Dean. Of course the death of the national teen idol set the American hype and pulp industry into hyperaction and within weeks, they'd turned out every imaginable memento and icon of Dean, from photo albums galore to a bust of Dean with a plastic surface described as "looks and feels like real skin."

At around the same time as the US began a series of large H-Bomb tests in the Pacific – which were televised rather like moon-shots in the sixties and during which thousands of troops were deliberately exposed to radiation in order to enable planners to see what a nuclear war might be like – another kind of bombshell arrived in Hibbing. It was a movie called *Blackboard Jungle*, starring Sydney Poitier, which was fairly mediocre. The movie was about tough city kids with education problems, but the kids weren't allowed to be real and the story was obvious drivel written down for the teen audience in the usual condescending way. However, the movie contained Bill Haley & the Comets performing a reasonably rousing version of *Rock Around The Clock*. Although they were an averagely exciting white band, they *were* a crucial catalyst for Rock 'n' Roll. *Rock Around The Clock* went to Number One and officially set the seal on the Rock 'n' Roll craze.

The film also contained some electrifying footage of another kind of rock 'n' roll; Little Richard doing *Tutti Frutti*, his first release and first hit. Richard Penniman, who took the name Little Richard, was to put it mildly, pretty wild. He was black, extremely handsome and loud. With hair arranged in a five-inch high quiff and clad in fantastic costume, he pounded on a piano while bouncing around and on it, and belted out *Tutti Frutti* in a voice that sounded as if it could cut concrete. Little Richard was the first absolutely "authentic" rock 'n' roller Bob Zimmerman had ever seen and he was immediately captivated. He bought all of Little Richard's records as they appeared.

*Tutti Frutti* reached No. 21 on the National Hit Parade. Chuck

Berry had a hit that fall too with *Maybellene*, which got to No. 5. All over the country there were dozens of good acts, rock 'n' rollers, who were gaining acceptance in a particular region. Elvis Presley, already a star in Tennessee, left Sun records for thirty-five thousand dollars and passed into the hands of Colonel Tom Parker.

The color bar in popular music, the bar against truly proletarian black music, was coming down. Then Elvis Presley burst into national prominence with *Heartbreak Hotel* at Number One and RCA discovered they'd signed a property that could sell as many records as almost the entire record industry had in 1950. The fault line was clear: Rock had broken the old guard's grip on popular taste. The kids, wild, young and pretty much innocent of sin, were a market force of their own.

Naturally enough, this shift in the geology of popular culture did not go unremarked. Fundamentalist Christian Preachers denounced it immediately and began organizing record burnings by the devout. They saw clearly the racial implications plus the appeal to pleasure, dancing, carnality and fun. All the things that, generally speaking, ensure one a ticket to hell.

Bob Zimmerman's response was to go home and practise being Little Richard on the piano. The piano was soon moved to the garage. Shortly he teamed up with a couple of friends and neighbors to form a group, the Golden Chords.

He haunted Crippa's record department, constantly ordering records that they never stocked. Rhythm 'n' Blues singles – the music he was tuning into nightly – material up from Memphis and Arkansas. Dispatch clerks working for those small labels, like Excello, Atlantic, Specialty must have all known and remarked on the fact that sales were booming in Northern Minnesota.

The Golden Chords were getting together a couple of times a week at Bob's house to listen to records, rock 'n' roll hits and Bob's already growing collection of rhythm 'n' blues. They'd play in the garage. (Monte Edwardson on guitar and Leroy Hoikkala, a neighborhood friend, on some drums.) Bob was strictly in control, it was rock à la Little Richard, from him screaming in a falsetto and them playing as directed.

Most of his peers however regarded him as a loner, someone who was a little aloof, perhaps shy, but certainly inner-directed. At the time, he was a chubby-faced kid with light brown hair cut, short back and sides with curls on top. He was no stand out in sports, nor was he terribly interested in school. Those who knew him said 'he didn't travel with any particular group of people. The kids he got involved with it was strictly for the music.'

Moreover, he was engaged in a stiff struggle for teenage personal autonomy at home. His parents were not entirely pleased with their son's passion for rock music. They refused to let him go out at nights and stay up late; they imposed curfews, negotiated limits, all of which he chafed at.

Working out with the Golden Chords had paid off though, since they were now doing a few gigs performing at local talent contests and local dances. They won few prizes but Bob felt the call of performing, there was a thrill in slamming out rock 'n' roll to an audience that he craved from then on.

Soon friends remarked: 'He was starting to really dig being a performer. Being up there on stage...'

He told everyone that rock 'n' roll music was 'meant for us, meant for the kids, it's ours.'

At about the same time, he was discovering that he had a severe geographical problem. Basically, he was growing up in the back of beyond. Hibbing and the other small towns of the Iron Range are strung out on a line along Highway 169, a slash of development in the northern forests. Thirty miles south and west lies the source of the Mississippi. All around are forests and the swarms of small and medium-sized lakes that characterize the glacially-eroded Laurentian shield country. To the North lies empty forest and lake country extending all the way to Churchill on Hudson Bay where the polar bears roam.

A couple of hour's drive south east lies Duluth and Superior, a small conurbation of one hundred and fifty thousand people. Two hundred miles to the south is Minneapolis St. Paul, a city of more than a million with a university and the administrative apparatus of State Government in St. Paul.

No one would ever have lived in Hibbing except for one thing, the Mesabi Iron deposits. Virtually laid bare by the scouring action of the ice sheet, these ores were rich and accessible. Endless trains, hundreds of cars long, ferried the ore down to Duluth where it was smelted and shipped to the steel towns of the mid-West to make everything from buildings to automobiles.

Hibbing grew swiftly, in step with the industrialization of the US at the end of the nineteenth century. Ten thousand or more miners were there, and by 1907, the infant Western Federation of Miners called for a strike for better wages. A bitter struggle ensued which the mining companies ended by shipping in seven thousand new immigrants from Eastern Europe. The

18

strike was broken and most of the first wave of miners left town. Eventually the new miners found the rule of the companies irksome enough to force them to strike towards the end of the First World War. There were several years of intermittent economic warfare and consequently, a permanent bitterness towards the companies crept into the work force.

These towns were only boom towns for a brief while. They were originally just encampments in the wilderness and the companies showed little concern for them. In 1918 the town of Hibbing was moved south a mile or so and the rich ore underneath was excavated. The result is a landmark, the "largest man made hole in the world" which covers a couple of thousand acres.

It was a strange little place to grow up. Many years later Dylan was to recall that strangeness:

> I was born in, grew up in a place so foreign that you had
> to be there to picture it. In the winter everything was
> still, nothing moved. Eight months of that. You can put it
> together. You can have some amazing hallucenogenic
> experiences doing nothing but looking out your window.
> There is also the summer, when it gets hot and sticky
> and the air is very metallic. There is a lot of Indian Spirit.
> The earth there is unusual, filled with ore. So there is
> something happening that is hard to define. There's a
> magnetic attraction there, maybe thousands and
> thousands of years ago some planet bumped into the
> land there. There is a great spiritual quality throughout
> the Mid West. Very subtle, very strong and that is where
> I grew up.

He also discovered the cultural limitations of a small town, heavily Catholic, very conservative, stuck way out in the boondocks. 'It was a narrow-minded sort of town' and 'it's a miracle that someone like Dylan came out of Hibbing', said contemporaries of his who also left the Iron Range.

The Hibbing teens were also pretty conservative, as most of them simply followed in their parents' footsteps. All that anybody professed to want was to get a job and a house and live like their parents lived.

At the talent contests where the Golden Chords played, Bob was usually depressed by the inevitable contest judging. The decision would always go to someone doing something traditional and conservative. Even when the audience screamed and danced while they played his Little Richard-style material, they always lost. He was too wild for Hibbing, too wild by half.

Along with the conservatism of a blue collar community there was the inevitable anti-semitism. In a town that was so overwhelmingly Catholic, the Zimmermans were rather unusual. Prejudice against jews existed although it wasn't voiced much. It hung there nonetheless. The country club was closed to them for example.

Robert discovered what it meant to be an outsider. Never to be part of the majority, only sure of acceptance on a certain level. They said he was touchy on the subject of his jewishness. Later, in Minneapolis and New York he would try and deny it altogether. The Catholic kids assured everyone, protestants and jews alike, that they were sure of going to hell because they weren't Catholic. His tendency towards aloofness and privacy was encouraged.

Nineteen fifty-six swept in with Elvis Presley dominating the Top Ten and the words Rock 'n' Roll on everybody's lips, whether in praise or damnation. That summer Bob was fifteen and he pestered his father until he was finally given a motorcycle – a Harley Davidson with a few years on it. That expanded his range and he bought a black leather jacket and cruised the Iron Range with friends like Leroy Hoikkala. Somehow he survived the young motorcyclist's usual close calls and near misses, although on one occasion he came within an ace of getting crushed by a freight train.

About this time, his father and his uncle expanded their business. They renamed the store; now it was Zimmerman's Furniture and Electric. The economic boom was still rolling. On the highways it was the golden age of gas guzzling. Gasoline cost thirty-five cents a gallon and cars were freaking out into a weird medley of lights, fins and contoured shapes. At White Sands and Cape Canaveral they were talking, within the new few years, of orbiting a satellite around the Earth. Jet aircraft were beginning to appear. Stereo sound was the coming thing and Rock 'n' Roll was booming.

Following hard on the heels of Presley and Little Richard came a host of rockers and the Top Ten was jumping to the new, heavy beat.

The Golden Chords broke up. Bob was leaning more and more heavily towards rhythm 'n' blues things he heard and wished to imitate. Leroy and Monte were happy with the rock 'n' roll hits.

Bob began taking the bus down to Minneapolis for visits to buy records. As soon as possible he started to borrow the family car and even rode his motorcycle down Highway 61 from Moose

Lake to St. Paul on these forays. He was sixteen and the world was expanding for him. Minneapolis was definitely where it was at. After the closed off world of Hibbing, the wider horizons down south were irresistible. He had already slipped shyly into the Dinkytown hangouts like the Ten O'Clock Scholar and knew all the record stores.

He soon had a new garage band, slightly bigger this time with four members. They were rock and jazz fans that he turned on to rhythm 'n' blues. Things began with his Little Richard impersonations on the piano and then moved on to other things. They performed together occasionally. The group was very loud; Bob screamed and sang in a falsetto and older members of their audiences were usually rather shocked by this strange phenomenon in their midst.

In his Sophomore year at High School, in October 1957, he met Echo Helstrom, a pretty blonde girl who was known to hang out with the town greasers and troublemaking element. He wasn't someone she would've considered even talking to before this, he'd been a "very clean cut, goody goody kid at the time. Plump and round-faced, not skinny like he became later. Baby-faced and quiet. I wouldn't have paid any attention to him because he was from the right side of the tracks and I was from the wrong side." Echo was from the proletarian section of town and to her Robert Zimmerman was decidedly middle class.

He was in the street, outside the Moose Lodge where he'd been playing with permission from the caretaker with his band. With him was John Buckland, a friend who shared his fascination for popular music like the blues. Echo and a girlfriend had been in a coffee shop; Bob and John Buckland tried to pick them up. Bob and Echo discovered they shared something unusual in common, 'You listen to Gatemouth Page!' he exclaimed. He was stunned. Immediately he pressed her to help him break back into the Moose Lodge which was now locked so he could do his Little Richard thing for her. She was too chicken to actually go in the Lodge and stood just by the door while he played.

Within a month they were going steady. He gave her his identity bracelet.

Echo's influence confirmed his drift towards greaserdom. Roaring around town on his Harley Davidson with Echo on the back, both of them in leather jackets, they looked like part of the town's pack of real greasers. The greasers were the unpopular town minority. In school teen society they were

21

nowhere, in fact they disdained school and rarely attended. They were troublemakers and were known to the police. For the most part they were working class.

Echo understood the difference, as she was later to say. 'He didn't fit in with the bums. I knew the real bums. All my friends were from the wrong side of the tracks. And Bob didn't fit in with them. He was a loner.' She also remembered fondly:

> We had a lot of great times together. He'd imagine the craziest things, act them out in his head and then we'd have to go and do them. He'd be quiet most of the time but when he got one of his crazy ideas his eyes would get so big and he'd carry on so. Everything had to be a big production for Bob, a big adventure.

Too slight to be a greaser, too middle-class to be accepted by the working class rebels and too weird to be part of high school society, Bob Zimmerman had become Hibbing's resident R&B freak.

Then in the early months of '58, he discovered Mrs Helstrom's old collection of Country & Western records. He dug into this new source of songs with his characteristic energy. He would listen intently to old sad tunes like *Ohio Prison Fire* and then go off with John Buckland to sit on the steps and play them on guitar.

He and Buckland were together a lot now and both were constructing a dream in which success as performing musicians, in the manner of the rock 'n' roll stars they could even see on TV now, was the only possible goal. Of course the chances of success in such a field were so slight that Robert Zimmerman's father saw this goal take a firm grip on his eldest boy with dread in his heart. There were several incidents at this time in which hostility between Bob and his father was obvious to his friends.

Robert had always helped out with the family business, and he had seen several facets of small business, including those sad scenes when home appliances bought on credit must be repossessed if the payments fail. The view of a future in that world of small business had no appeal for him. In fact, he couldn't even consider it. There was some bitterness and unease between father and son from this point on.

However, there was to be no turning back now. According to Echo Helstrom, he was already looking for a stage name, a new persona. In the spring of '58 he told her that he was going to call himself Bob Dylan.

Where he got the name, why he chose Dylan, have become controversies of the distant past. He claimed on different occasions that he took the name from a (non-existent) uncle

who was a gambler in Las Vegas and whose name was Dillon
– which he altered – and again that he made it up on the spur
of the moment in the Ten O'Clock Scholar in Minneapolis when
he needed a performing name. Throughout dozens of hostile
interviews he resolutely refused to acknowledge that he'd
borrowed it from Dylan Thomas, the Welsh Poet who died of
alcoholism in New York City. Of course, there is that line in
*Hard Rain's A Gonna Fall* concerning a "poet who died in the
gutter" but although it seems likely that Bob Zimmerman saw
the name Dylan in connection with Dylan Thomas, it also seems
that he was never very much interested in Thomas's poetry and
had never read any of it. In 1978 he said:

> I haven't read that much of Dylan Thomas. It's a
> common thing to change your name. It isn't that
> incredible. Many people do it.

Having a name was one thing; keeping a rock 'n' roll band
going was another:

> You couldn't make it back then in rock 'n' roll. You
> couldn't carry around an amplifier and electric guitar and
> expect to survive.

Certainly not in Northern Minnesota, where there are just ten
towns to seek out gigs in. To take a band on the road was
economically unfeasible for the few gigs available within five
hundred miles and without a band, young Zimmerman and
Buckland were stranded.

On the radio they could hear the new rock 'n' roll brigade
cutting up the charts; Jerry Lee Lewis, Buddy Holly & the
Crickets, heck even Bobby Darin was having hits. That summer,
a piece of nonsense by Sheb Wooley called *The Purple People Eater*
sold a million and topped the charts for six weeks in between
Elvis Presley's hits. The world was passing them by, but there
was little that could be done about it.

That spring, Bob discovered the work of John Steinbeck and
read such books as *Cannery Row* and *Grapes Of Wrath*. Echo
Helstrom recalled that his enthusiasm became a mania and in a
short time he read all the Steinbeck he could find.

Not long afterwards he heard a record by Odetta, a black
folksinger. It was very important:

> The first thing that turned me onto folksinging was
> Odetta. I heard a record of hers in a record store, when
> you could listen to records there in the store. That was in
> '58.

He was bored with the limited world of Hibbing and eager
to escape. While still playing occasionally with a group in

Duluth, he was turning more and more to Folk music as an outlet and a possible way out of Northern Minnesota:

> I became interested in folk music because I had to make it somehow. Obviously I'm not a hardworking cat. I played the guitar, that's all I did.'

In the meantime, Elvis had been drafted into the US army and a new crop of clean cut teen idols was being promoted for the new becoming teenage market.

That summer, he spent most of his time down in Minneapolis and Duluth, neglecting Echo. She soon made up her mind to end their relationship, since he wasn't interested anymore and shortly after the resumption of classes in the Autumn, she gave him back his ID bracelet.

His Senior Year at Hibbing High was a time of slow, torturous boredom. He was uninterested in school, not very eager to learn the Zimmerman business and desperate to get out of there and go someplace exciting. His weekends were devoted to music, searching for records, going to see those performers that trekked that far north to play and playing himself whenever possible. He was seriously discontented, hating the feeling that he was marking time, circling uselessly, when he ought to be far away learning new songs and experiencing the world.

He graduated in the summer of 1959 and beneath his photo in the school classbook he put simply, "Robert Zimmerman, gone to join Little Richard."

# CHAPTER TWO

# Dinkytown

In the autumn of '59, Bob Zimmerman came down Highway 61 once more to Minneapolis. He enrolled at the University of Minnesota Arts School on a state scholarship. In what may have been a concession to his parents, he had abandoned the greaser uniform for the collegiate one. He wore corduroys (this was the year that saw blue jeans banned in schools across the nation), and button-down shirts and white bucks. He was vain enough not to wear glasses, although he was myopic enough to need them; he squinted a lot instead. He moved into the Jewish Fraternity House on campus, Sigma Alpha Mu, and started attending classes.

He was finally out of Hibbing, finally away from his family and his father's disapproving eye. He soon found he had nothing in common with his fellow Fratmen. They later recalled that he was unfriendly, aloof, even surly.

Almost immediately he headed down to Dinkytown, to the bohemian haunts, the coffee shops and student bars that lurked there. He knew Minneapolis pretty well by now and, during the summer, he'd prepared himself for this new stage. He'd been listening to more "authentic" folksingers, like Sara Ogun Gunning and Woody Guthrie. He had his guitar and harmonica with him and in Dinkytown, he found the people he now needed – the poets, the folkies, the old leftists and the new leftists, the Kerouac age beatniks, the writers and professional intellectuals.

The Dinkytown coffee houses were their natural habitat. The Ten O'Clock Scholar on 14th Street, a block from the Campus, was perhaps the best known hangout. By early October Bob was primed with enough songs to try his hand at playing for the customers in the Scholar in the front window on the little four inch-high stage.

It was certainly *the* time to be getting into Folk music. Rock had been partially co-opted by the professional image builders of Tin Pan Alley, the music was softening and losing its urgency. For students there was now a quickening revival in folk forms, the blues, white traditional music and the new popular hits from such acts as the Kingston Trio.

In Cambridge, near Harvard University, there was Club 47 and a strong folk music scene. A very young Joan Baez was one of the local star turns there with her thrilling voice.

In New York there were recording contracts – serious folk musicians were actually cutting records to be released on new folk music labels like Folkways and Vanguard. Pop folk had cracked the charts. Harry Belafonte had taken it on TV and the Kingston Trio had gone from the Purple Onion coffee house in San Francisco to Number One on the best-sellers for a week in '58 and sold more than a million copies of *Tom Dooley*.

Elsewhere on the spectrum were the Weavers headed by Pete Seeger, who were the vanguard for those interested in socially concerning and arousing songs. Beyond the Weavers lay the grand old tradition and the likes of Woody Guthrie, a great institution of American Folk Music.

Pete Seeger was in trouble with the McCarthyites and was in the process of being dragged before Congressional hearings, something that was to lead to his being blacklisted from network TV.

Woody Guthrie lay ill, slowly dying of Huntingdon's Chorea out at Greystone Hospital, in New Jersey. He'd been there since early '59 after being transferred from Brooklyn State Hospital. The disease had first struck in 1951 and slowly it had robbed him of the ability to play or sing. Some diehard fans of his, Bob and Sidsel Gleason, heard that Woody was in Greystone and they offered to take him to their house at weekends. Soon the Gleason's house on weekends was filled with the folksinging fraternity (it was extremely male dominated at that time) and East Orange, New Jersey became a recording center of some importance, as Bob Gleason taped the impromptu hootenannies that would take place while Woody's friends sang to him.

The Ten O'Clock Scholar was another sign of the burgeoning folk movement. Starting with Greenwich Village in New York, and a couple of spots in San Francisco and Los Angeles, folk clubs, folk atmosphere coffee houses and the like had spread rapidly across the land. Early in the year David Lee had bought the place and rejuvenated it and initiated the policy of having singers in the front window. It didn't make much money though – there wasn't enough turnover and with coffee at only twenty cents a cup there wasn't room for much profit margin.

At the Scholar, Bob was Bob Dylan. The Zimmerman identity he left behind on campus and in the Frat house. His initial efforts at folksinging were hard to appreciate. He sang in a nasal monotone and did his best with a traditional folk style that really didn't suit his voice. Customers often thought at first that he was placed there to make sure they didn't linger at the tables for more than a cup or two of coffee. People complained to the owner who occasionally asked Bob to sing quietly. Soon enough, Lee tired of the unequal task of squeezing a profit out of the place and sold it, around the end of '59.

About the same time, John Koerner returned to Minneapolis after a stint in the US Marines. Koerner was a fixture in the local folkscene. Later, with his friends Dave Ray and Tony Glover, he was to achieve some success in the trio Koerner, Ray and Glover, who released several country-tinged folk albums in the sixties.

Koerner met Dylan at the Scholar soon afterwards:

> At this time he was just strumming, mostly chords and like that. He was doing standard folk songs. But I do remember him singing some of his own stuff too. He was beginning to write his own material.

Other friends from that time later commented:

> He just wanted to get into a situation where he could learn, where his talent and his feel for the music could develop. He learned things quickly and developed at a remarkable speed. But those first few months he was nowhere at all. Just a kid trying damned hard to learn.

John Koerner and Bobby played and hung around together at the Scholar and the new Purple Onion over in St. Paul, near Hamline University. Bob soon abandoned the neat clothing he'd brought down from Hibbing and took to wearing the standard folkie uniform of the time: work shirts, boots, jeans. He stopped bothering to feed people his old line of self-aggrandizing myth, in which he had been a near successful rock 'n' roller up in Duluth, "had been on TV" and done backing for Bobby Vee. Instead, all his stories and fables now had an Okie ring to them. When he went up to Hibbing to visit his parents he just disappeared from Dinkytown without a word and claimed after returning that he'd just been down to Oklahoma or somewhere else that was romantic and far away.

Another lesson in folksinging was the commercial aspect of

things. At the Scholar and the Purple Onion he was getting two dollars a night. Two dollars to play folk songs for three or four hours. Of course, coffee was only twenty cents a cup and he had few personal needs other than cigarettes and food, but he was already learning new lessons.

The new owners of the Scholar, Clark Batho and Bob Fishman, initially put an end to the nightly singing but trade dropped off and complaints were voiced, so they became convinced that the student customers actually wanted that stuff. They offered Bob three bucks a night to leave the Purple Onion and come back to the Scholar. He accepted and stayed for months. This was his classroom; in fact, sometime in January 1960, he just about stopped going to college at all. His Zimmerman identity was left hanging on a peg at the Frat house and he avoided school and anyone who knew his real identity. Of course, there were those who knew who he was and took the trouble to tell anyone who'd listen about the secret identity of the young folksinger working so constantly at the Scholar.

Batho and Fishman were now charging fifty cents cover charge at the Scholar and this aroused hard feelings among some old habitués. Hugh Brown, guitar player, poet, a friend of Dylan's and an English Major at the university recalled:

> Nobody liked Clark much. When the Scholar was first started it was a very comfortable place. You could go in and sit around all day. But Clark wanted more turnover and he made us all very angry. He took away what we considered our place.

Bob was growing his hair a little longer; he'd discovered that he could charm the daylights out of girls and he was hardly ever going back to the Frat house. Indeed, he finally moved out of there after coming under some pressure from the Frat men to conform and get down to some studying and took a dingy, partially furnished room above Gray Drugs on the corner of 4th Street and 14th Avenue. Just a half block down the street from the Scholar, his commute was now a lot shorter. However, he did continue to attend classes sporadically but with no serious intent in mind. His learning place was Dinkytown and he was putting himself through a heavy course of intensive study every other night on stage at the Scholar.

At this time the people he met were almost unanimously impressed with one thing, he had *Charisma*. Explained Gretel Hoffman who went with him for a while before marrying David Whittaker, one of the leading lights of the Dinkytown intellectual hip establishment:

> When I first met Bobby, he claimed he was a real Okie. He never talked about Steinbeck because Bobby was, at least superficially, non-intellectual, a primitive. He sort of *was* one of Steinbeck's characters. He had a whole set of original stories that he was an Okie, that he was an orphan...

Although he hung out with Hugh Brown and other intellectual hips with Marxist ideas and radical dreams, he wasn't actively participating in their discourse. Some who knew him then and disliked him saw him as a poseur, someone hanging left but thinking only of himself with no intention of contributing to the hot and worthy discussions of political and social concern that Dinkytown was full of. This is no doubt at least partially true. Dylan was nurturing his talent, trying to feel the extent of it. He was beginning to feel that he had *something*, but what it was... he wasn't exactly sure yet.

His friends, like Hugh Brown and David Morton, recalled that his stories were easy to penetrate after a while. They realized that he was not some orphan Okie. Eventually they learned he was Zimmerman and came from little Hibbing. Yet they found it easy to ignore the fables – Bob was too enjoyable, radiating adolescent charm that proved very winning, especially on stage.

He'd started to impress his audiences. He had regulars who loved his stuff. He still couldn't sing so good but as Clark Batho sourly noted: 'He thought he was a real monkey show' because he would fiddle with harmonica holders and guitar strings and keep the audience laughing with asides and jokes.

He was relatively uninterested in reading or politics, at least from outward appearances. He was driving towards becoming a full-fledged primitive folk artist, just taking his vision and using whatever material came along to express it.

Kevin McGosh who owned the local radical bookstore where various types of leftists were known to gather and debate said of Dylan:

> He never had any part in the radical ideas. It wasn't only that he didn't read any books, but he seemed completely oblivious to everything except music. He didn't know about radicalism. He had contact with all these people but he didn't know it at all.

Of course, McCosh was of an older generation, who'd known

the thirties and held the history of the left in their memories. They had little use for someone who was trying to respond naturally, anti-intellectually in fact, to the world of 1960, while at the same time steeping himself in folk song from the past. He'd taken a deep dive into the poetic world of folk song myth, and had been aiming that way since the days of Gatemouth Page anyway, and now he was in so deep that there wasn't room for anything else. And besides, he had to hone up his stage act. McCosh and the others who disliked Dylan were immune to his sense of humor, and it was that crackling, blazing sense of humor that drew his friends so tight. He was the perfect antidote for the gloom that could fall upon young radicals who did contemplate the grotesquely slow pace of change. Here Cuba had had a revolution at last and in the US, blacks were still being denied spaces at lunch counters and the like. America's primitive social arrangements were hard to live with and equally hard to imagine changing. Dylan seemed to act as a lightning rod for humor for them and thus was indispensable.

David Whittaker was an important friend and an influence on Dylan. Dylan later told Anthony Scaduto: 'I saw Whittaker and it was like that', motioning as with a karate chop 'just over and out. I was on this side and suddenly I was on that side. Whittaker mostly, but also Brown and Morton and the others. You see they were incredible, they were just incredible. The way they were living, the way they thought, nobody was doing it like them. There just wasn't anyone around like them. Especially David.

Dylan had found the friends, the upper classmen of hip virtually, and without showing much sign of it he proceeded to absorb a lot from them, ideas, books even, and a sense of the world and its ills. Whittaker said:

> I think I had an understanding of where Bob's mind was. We were on the same wavelength. There was something about his view of the world, a radical view combined with a sense of humor. And getting more like humorous, we spent a great deal of time laughing at the world.

He had also dropped the Kingston Trio and Harry Belafonte type of stuff from his playlist. He'd never really enjoyed those things anyway, now he was using more authentic material; Woody Guthrie, for example, and he found that it suited his playing style better too.

He asked Batho for a raise. He was told he wasn't worth five dollars a night. Why? 'Your attitude. It's bad enough at three dollars. It'll be impossible at five dollars.'

Bob stormed over to the Purple Onion near Hamline and got taken on at six dollars a night. Batho later spoke of Dylan's temperamental performances some nights at the Scholar:

> Bobby was a prima donna, very temperamental. If the crowd wasn't listening to him, wasn't appreciating him, he would get mad and yell at the customers to shut up. If they complained about it or refused to comply with the orders from the stage he'd stomp off and go down to the basement and smoke a cigarette, grumbling about the customers the whole time.

What Batho dismissed as a mere "monkey show" however was an important development for Dylan. He'd found a way to work up a physical relationship with an audience, a link over which he could communicate a lot, even charisma.

Many who saw him perform at this time noted that he quickly developed a shy, Chaplinesque stage charm. He would clown a little for the audience and it worked. Despite later denials of Chaplin's influence, he did confess to it in an early interview in August 1961:

> If I'm on stage, my idols, even my biggest idol, when I'm on stage is Charlie Chaplin. And uh, it's uh well it takes a while to explain it but I'd say he's one of THE men.

Of course he was right. As Bob Zimmerman, he'd realized that in a league filled with such teen idols and watered down imitations of James Dean and Elvis as Fabian and Frankie Avalon, there was just no future in rock 'n' roll. To appeal to folk music fans required a different body language, one that stressed charm. Chaplin's technique, using a physical humor built on charm, fragility and a recurring sense of impending disaster that was always just recovered at the edge of doom, was a good one for a young folksinger. He was the india-rubber performer, no matter how his instruments, his song list, or the room and his employer bugged him, he would bounce back and get on with the next song.

Gretel Hoffman put it simply, 'He had a delightful sense of humor.'

In the early summer of 1960, Dylan was offered a job playing piano in a honky tonk out in Central City, Colorado. Central City was 'an historic recreation of the old West' town, complete with outlaws and cowboys who fired caps from authentic looking guns for the tourists. He told hardly anyone about it and one day simply disappeared.

That summer in the Gilded Garter, Bob played piano for a few dollars a night. He was living with a stripper in a hotel down a mile or so from the tourist trap saloon. Speaking to friends afterwards of that summer job, he would exclaim:

> Jesus, what a job. Hey they had strippers and all kind of things. Had to play between some real weird people.

Back in Dinkytown that fall he was playing more Woody Guthrie songs. Before this, Guthrie had been just one of many folksinger sources for Bob; now Guthrie became very important. It seems that the vital spark was applied by David Whittaker who gave Bob a copy of Guthrie's book *Bound For Glory* to read. They'd been listening to the songs of *Dust Bowl Ballads* at the time and when Whittaker found Dylan hadn't read it, he scouted around town for one. Finally, one was found in a University faculty member's bookshelf and Bob read it and was immediately entranced.

The life he had been imagining for himself, the background on the highways and byways, the life in the "Dusty old Fairgrounds", that life was Woody Guthrie's life. It was right there, the story of a folksinger surviving the Depression while writing a wealth of folk songs that have become standards.

After reading Guthrie's book, Dylan was drawn like a moth to the flame to Guthrie's music. Whittaker remembered Bob playing *Tom Joad* on the phonograph, "and he'd play it all day long, that half hour song. All day long, all day. Day after day."

Dylan himself commented: "I was pretty fanatical about what I wanted to do."

He set down and learned "about two hundred of Woody's songs".

Soon he was so Guthrie-struck that people would make fun of him at parties if he got drunk. He was very impressionable when he was in his cups. People would start telling him that Woody was there, that he'd come to Dinkytown, that he was even downstairs. Dylan would stumble out into the street foolishly calling for Woody. Everyone else would laugh themselves silly.

'He was so painfully sincere', recalled one friend from that time.

'He absolutely became Woody Guthrie for three months.'

It seemed that Bob had found his thesis subject for the second year of his own self-imposed course in folksinging. As usual, when he took to something, he became absolutely maniacal about it until it was totally consumed and understood.

He had no real place to live now, as winter was coming on, and he had no wish to go back to Hibbing for the time being. He kept saying: "We're going to New York to see Woody."

The urge to go and see Woody was enough to get him seriously thinking about really going to New York.

In November he decided to take his stuff on the road and see what he could do with it. He travelled to Chicago first, hitching on the highway. He stayed there with a friend he'd met while playing in the Honky Tonk in Central City, Colorado. Then he met a girl and moved in with her, typical folksinger style. He stayed for a couple of weeks and moved through university circles, parties, coffee houses, even dorms, playing whenever possible.

He was also writing; he wrote *Song To Woody*, his tribute to the idol who was dying in New Jersey.

He was still slightly unsure though of which direction to take. He left Chicago in mid-January and headed up to Madison, Wisconsin, another mid-west university town. There he unpacked himself on someone and immediately started playing for anyone who'd sit still long enough to listen.

He impressed some of those who saw him, although others recalled that his Woody Guthrie accent sounded "as phony as shit" and others were angered by his insistence on playing one Guthrie song after another, all night long, thus ruining parties where they wanted to discuss politics. When he told people he was going to Greenwich Village in New York, they thought he was "doomed", he looked so young, so frail and basically still so incompetent that everyone was convinced that he would simply "be eaten alive" in New York.

After a few days playing here and there in Madison and sleeping on floors, he left Wisconsin and set out for the East. He arrived in New York at the end of January 1961. It was freezing cold – a foot of snow had arrived the week before and the city was huge and grey and just a little ominous.

# CHAPTER THREE

# New York

Dylan got to the Big Apple – as so many have done – with little more than his guitar, clothes and a trembling self-assurance. He went straight downtown to the Village and soon found the Cafe Wha?, a coffee house on MacDougal Street.

From the very first moments it seems, the interaction between Bob Dylan and New York City had an exhilarating, near-hallucinatory quality. He was nineteen years and seven months old, impressionable but already wise, soaked in the mythic language of folk-song and Woody Guthrie.

At Cafe Wha? he begged for a chance to play – an orphanish waif out of the freezin' winter's murk who was truly desperate. He played...

"So they gave me a dollar to play in the Hootenanny, no in fact it came to a dollar fifty. And I played there and they really flipped. They really did. So I figured if they liked me so much that maybe someone would have a place to stay that night. So I asked from the stage and about four hands went up. So my buddy and I, we sort of went and checked 'em all and picked out a fellow. He was with a girl. And my buddy says to me, 'you don't look so hot', that's what he said. He said, 'he looks pretty gay' (laughs) and I said, 'uh, I didn't know anything about that kind of stuff' – well I knew anyway, he was with a girl. And so we went with him. And the girl got off at 34th street and we got off at 42nd street. Well, we went in a bar first before we went to find a place to stay and we met his friend Dora. Dora was his friend who stayed with him. And we all went to a party. And THAT was my first night in New York."

Again, sometime later, with further benefit from hindsight, Dylan recounted the tale in a verse in a talking blues, *Talking Folklore Center* which was dedicated to Israel Young's Folklore Center in Greenwich Village:

I came down to New York Town,

> Got out and started walking around,
> It's up around sixty second street,
> All of a sudden a cop on his beat
> Said my hair was too long – said my boots were too dirty
> Said my hat was un-American, said he'd throw me in
> jail.
> So I got on a subway and took a seat
> Got out on forty second street,
> I met this fellow named Delores there
> He started rubbin' his hands through my hair.
> I figured something was wrong, so I ran through ten hot
> dog stands, four movie houses and a couple of dancing
> studios to get back to the subway train...

Whatever else may have happened on those first couple of days he picked himself up and dusted himself off and bussed or hitched out to Greystone Hospital in Morristown, New Jersey, to see Woody.

Guthrie's condition by then had grown very serious. He could barely talk, could only just manage to strum a chord on a guitar, he was very hard to understand. But Dylan sat with Guthrie for a long time, and Bobby had been listening to this man's recorded voice with an intense amount of attention for many months. He talked with Woody and explained himself a little, and he played for the old man too. Guthrie, there is no doubt about this, was charmed. He saw at once that there was something in this wispy little kid that was different. He gladly accepted the devotion offered by the boy and, in return, his touch legitimized Bob Dylan with a very special circle of friends.

On the last weekend in that freezing January, Dylan hitch-hiked out to the Gleason's apartment in East Orange and talked his way inside. Most of that Sunday afternoon he sat on the floor by the couch where Guthrie lay. He didn't talk much, he kept his hat on, but he communicated with Guthrie. He sang for Woody and that night after he'd gone back to the city, Woody remarked: 'He's a talented boy. Gonna go far.'

Here it must be recalled that Guthrie was never overly generous in his praise of his fellows. Pete Seeger and Jack Elliott, for example, he dismissed as "singers of folk songs, not folksingers." The boy however, was something else. "But that Bobby Dylan is a folksinger" he said, "Oh Christ, he's a folksinger all right."

Bob sent cards back to Dinkytown, to David Whittaker; "people clap for me", he bragged.

From the earliest recorded evidence – Dylan's tapes of his

basic set at this time – it's difficult really to know why they would have. The Minneapolis Tape from 1960, which has appeared recently on the Dylanophile market, has songs like *Muleskinner Blues, Streets of Glory, Red Rosy Bush* and *Johnny I Hardly Knew You*, plus some Talking blues things like *Talkin' Hugh Brown Blues*. Basically Bob, at this point, was just another of a whole legion of would-be folksingers that were tramping the streets of cities like New York, London and San Francisco.

Yet from almost his first few performances, in the early evenings before the paid singers in the coffee houses, he aroused some interest. This was especially true of the female section of the Village folk music audience. A little fragile looking, yet clearly possessing a Huck Fin ragamuffin soul, Bob was angelic enough to set hearts a-beating all over the place. Leftist, middle-aged, frequently Jewish, Village women were desperately eager to mother him and take care of him.

He also excited powerful interests in younger female folkies, and this early female interest stirred controversy and a little disgust among the male folksinging fraternity. Yet somehow or other he always managed to find a bed for the night and the necessary meals. When all else failed, he would crash in a dormlike apartment over on East 5th street.

The following weekend, after visiting Guthrie in East Orange again, he wrote *Song To Woody*, a distillation of his feelings at that time.

"It was written in the 1960th winter", he later told Sing Out! "In New York City in the drug store on the 8th street. It was on one of them freezing days that I came back from Sid and Bob Gleason's in East Orange New Jersey. Woody was there that day and it was a February Sunday night... And I just thought about Woody; I wondered about him, thought harder and wondered harder. I wrote this song in five minutes..."

He'd been going out to the hospital every other day in the week, and at the Gleason's he was meeting the other members of Guthrie's intimate circle, Jack Elliott, Cisco Houston, Pete Seeger, Will Geer, all long-established names in the senior class of folk musicians. Dylan reportedly got along very well with Cisco Houston, who unbeknownst to all, was dying of cancer. He continued to play and perform almost to the end when, abruptly, he went home to San Bernadino in April of that year, to die.

Commented Ramblin' Jack Elliott: "Cisco never showed the white feather." But he did show the youngster from the midwest a friendly face and in general, Bob was quickly accepted among this august group.

Of course he continued to paint a vast tapestry of wild inventions about his own past. Mostly he said he was an orphan, that he'd grown up following the circuses around on those 'Dusty Old Fairgrounds'. He must have seemed a splendid apparition to Guthrie and Houston. An intensely charismatic and intelligent kid who had completely mastered the Guthrie style and was obviously going to use it to develop his own thing very soon.

While visiting the Gleason's, he was also caught on tape. Some of that tape has long been in use in the bootleg Dylan market and although most of it is not of particularly good quality, there is a solid version of *San Francisco Bay Blues*.

The rest of the time was spent hanging out in the twilight world of poverty, urban adventure and night-time living that characterized apprenticeship in folk music in the early sixties. Of these early weeks, Dylan was later to say:

> I bummed around, I dug it all – the streets and the snows
> and the starving and the five flight walk-ups and
> sleeping in rooms with ten people. I dug the trains and
> the shadows, the way I dug the ore mines and coal
> mines. I just jumped right to the bottom of New York.

And yet despite being chronically broke, since he wasn't getting paid for playing in clubs yet, he gained good marks from those he crashed on. Mrs. Gleason once enthused:

> One thing about that child I loved – if there was snow to
> be shovelled, he shovelled; if there were dishes to wash,
> he washed dishes. Bobby didn't bum.

As people got to know him a little better, they soon began to realize that he was not really what he claimed to be. His stories were so loose and so continuously updated with new additions and new names (even the names of blues singers dead for generations), that he claimed to have met and learned songs from, that most people realized he was hiding something else, like a middle-class background.

This annoyed some people intensely. By and large they were the same people who seriously *cherished* folk music in its ancient forms, who rubbed the lamp on an antique art and were horrified by the charisma and sexual charm this freaky kid was exercising on the female contingent of the folk music audience in the Village.

These people were never destined to become fans of Bob Dylan. However, many of them continue to devote their lives to folk music, even today.

Objections from this group fell on deaf ears. Within a month or so there had formed a definite cadre of Dylan fans, largely female, that followed him around the Village from coffee shop to folk music club.

He tried to get into one of the Monday night hootenannies held by Mike Porco, the owner of Gerde's Folk City; the "hoots" were an opportunity for young unknowns to get on stage before a larger audience than was available in the clubs. Mondays were always packed out at Gerde's and Porco had plenty of performers lined up. He sent Bob away the first time, unsure whether he was old enough.

People started telling Porco that Dylan was pretty good, that he really ought to give him a chance. So he told Bob to get some proof of his age and come back. Dylan returned within a week with some ID. Of course it bore the name Zimmerman. Porco thought nothing of it, everyone had a stage name. Ramblin' Jack Elliott was actually one Elliott Adnopoz, son of a Jewish doctor and a native of Brooklyn.

Finally he got his chance and from the start, he did well at Gerde's. The late night crowd saw something special in him. He impressed many, delighted some. Porco however didn't see it yet: It was just another person that came in and performed.

> Then he started to come in every Monday; I don't think
> he missed a Monday, and a few people liked him. They
> started to call my attention to him; they said: 'that kid is
> pretty good.'

Dave Van Ronk, an established folk-blues performer tagged him:

> He was something of a *natural* (my emphasis) – a cat who
> seems to know all the rules and systematically breaks
> them. He gave the appearance of not knowing anything,
> but you could just feel he knew what it was all about,
> and he was deliberately breaking the rules and making it
> work.

Other performers also saw that he was well used to a stage and they saw the calculated risks he took in marrying something from Chaplin to his "pixie-runt" Huck Finn character that sang talkin' blues.

Moreover, the "monkey show" from Minneapolis was now honed to an effective tool for getting an audience on his side.

Still, he was cautious at first. "Bob wasn't reaching out for the audience then", said one who was there. He only played after the midnight break, when the high school kids and the "straights" would go home. Then Gerde's filled up with folkies and Villagers. This crowd tended to look down on the earlier one, many of them were performers themselves and the Monday night hoots were very much a showcase of performers for performers at this time.

Bob was not only performing however, he was absorbing. Here in New York he didn't need to start a conversation to get other people talking about something interesting. Here everything was exploding; the Village was filled with a sense of expectancy; hundreds of people from all over the country, the whole world, were working in lower Manhattan to bring about change. For the most part they had no idea whatsoever of what they were doing. Dylan later described the scene thus:

> Washington Square was a place where people you knew or met congregated every Sunday and it was a world of music... there could be twenty different things happening in the same kitchen or in the same park; there could be two hundred bands in one park in New York; there could be fifteen jug bands, five bluegrass bands and an old crummy string band, twenty Irish Confederate groups, a Southern Mountain band, folksingers of all kinds and colors, singing John Henry work songs. There were bodies piled sky-high doing whatever they felt like doing. Bongo drums, conga drums, saxophone players, xylophone players, drummers of all nations and nationalities; poets who would rant and rave from the statues. You know those things don't happen anymore. But then it was what was happening...

In fact, he was in the midst of the best folksinging milieu in the world. It was right there and this was his most important semester. It was only a year since he'd left the fraternity house for good, "when they tried to make me join," but already by comparison, his previous life seemed light years away.

During these days, he visited Israel Young's Folklore Center a lot. It was a good place to practise, to try things out on a knowledgeable audience. Young recalled that Dylan didn't really listen to anybody else:

> He was very powerful right away, took over the room right away. Very competitive... Bob Dylan was performing all the time.
>
> What I'm saying is that he wasn't an innocent kid when he came to New York City. He knew exactly what he wanted, knew how to use people and when the point came that he didn't have to use them any more, he

dropped them.

The winter ground out; Bob bummed, played for dimes and nickels and stuck it out. Friends kept on at Mike Porco who started to listen to some of Dylan's own things, the words. "He musta been at the hoot night twenty times or more". Porco later told Ratso Slocum:

> When I spoke to him and said, 'Bobby I know you would like to work here. Maybe we can get you a job.' And his eyes almost popped out of his head, and he said, 'Oh yes, man, anytime.'

Porco decided to put him on in April with John Lee Hooker. Bob virtually jumped out of his shoes; this was his first real paying gig in New York; his first performance before a real Gerde's audience other than the hoot crowd on Mondays. Even better, he knew Hooker would pull a big crowd, being as he was one of the most popular black blues singers then performing.

First though he had to join the union; Porco took care of it:

> I knew Bob didn't have a cabaret card or belong to the union, so I put him into the union. I took him up there and I pay for the card. I think it was eighty dollars or something. At the union they asked how old he was and he said twenty and the guy says if he was only twenty he gotta bring somebody from his family to sign the contract, to come back tomorrow with the contract. So Bob said, 'I ain't got no mother', so the guy says, 'OK come back with your father! And Bobby says, 'I ain't got no father either.' So the guy looked at me and said, 'What are we gonna do? I can't put him in the union unless... Mike you want to sign for him? So I asked Bob and he said he'd appreciate it, so I had to sign as his guardian.

With Cabaret card in hand, he started practising hard during the first week of April. Every night he went to see Hooker who had begun a three-week stint. Bob was due to open for Hooker for the last two weeks of his stint.

On top of the usual nerves accompanying such a first night in New York, Dylan was also worried about a backlash among the folk crowd. Here he was the unknown from Minnesota, only in New York two and a half months, and he was getting a big break. Would the others turn against him?

Friends and fans packed into Gerde's that night and Dylan did a five-song set, very brief it seemed; a couple of Guthrie numbers, a black blues and a version of the *House of the Rising*

*Sun* that was pretty similar to Dave Van Ronk's, plus of course *Song To Woody*. Alas, no tape of this has come to light, but his friends gave him an enthusiastic reception, cheering loudly at the end, when he jumped off stage and ran over to pump Bob Gleason's hand, thanking him for support.

The next two weeks were vital for Bob Dylan. He was seen by a number of people who would soon become important in his life, like Joan Baez who recalled him as seeming "tiny, just tiny, with that goofy little hat on. And he was just astounding, I was totally absorbed..."

At the end of his Gerde's gig, Bob went to stay with the Gleason's in East Orange for a few days before travelling up to Branford, Connecticut, for the Indian Neck Folk Festival. This was held on May 6 at the Montewese Hotel, and a tape of Dylan singing a couple of Guthrie songs was made and preserved. However, sound quality – as with so many bootlegs and fragments of this kind – is very poor. In fact if you didn't know it was Dylan you might not guess it from listening. However, it does show that Dylan was still working in the Guthrie vein, plus doing Leadbelly-type blues.

Towards the end of May, around his birthday, he went home to Minnesota. He turned up in Dinkytown and played in a memorable hoot. His performance was caught on a tape known generally as The Minnesota Party Tape, which contains tracks like *Man Of Constant Sorrow, Pretty Polly, This Land Is Your Land, Wild Mountain Thyme, This Train, San Francisco Bay Blues* and some talking blues as well.

Paul Nelson and Jon Pankake, who edited the Little Sandy Review, a folk music quarterly, noted how much Dylan had grown during his first sojourn in New York.
In a mere half year he had learned to churn up exciting, bluesy, hard-driving harmonica and guitar music, and had absorbed during his visits with Guthrie, not only the great Okie musician's unpredictable syntax, but his very vocal color, diction and inflection.

Dylan's performance that spring evening was hectic and shaky, but it contained all the elements of the now perfected performing style "that has made him the most original newcomer to folk music", they were later to write.

Dylan got back to New York in June and resumed his new life. His housing problem was solved when some people named McKenzie took him in. He slept in their son's room on and off through the summer while the son was at camp. He also hung out at Dave and Terry Van Ronk's place a lot and often slept over, and he continued to appeal to female folkies of all ages.

Later in the month he went up to Boston to check out the scene in Cambridge, home of Club 47, where Joan Baez had first come to prominence. However, he was still unknown outside of Village circles really and was just too freaky, with his Guthrie songs and unorthodox stage manner, to get a chance to play.

He was writing his own songs, as the writing bug had bitten him deeply by this time. At the McKenzie's he'd sit down late at night and work things out on yellow legal pad. He was always carrying around scraps of paper with ideas on them. Out of things like news stories on page five of the Daily News he conjured up songs, bizarre little beauties like *Talking Bear Mountain Massacre Blues*, one of the earliest.

*Talking Bear* told of a disastrous outing by a Harlem Social Club that was supposed to steam up to Bear Mountain picnic grounds, north of the city on the Hudson River. Due to a fake ticket sale panic however, the trip exploded into a three-ring fistfight and ended in chaos at the dock in Manhattan.

Dylan sang at the Commons, the Cafe Wha? and the Gaslight too and, on occasions, he would get a share from the hat that was passed around the crowd to augment the meager wages of the performers – typically ten or fifteen dollars for several hours of playing. On Mondays he went to the hoots and played in the company of the other young professionals of the Village, like Paul Clayton, Tom Paxton, Dave Van Ronk, Jack Elliott, Judy Collins and others like Phil Ochs who were also starting out, fresh from college in the midwest, to try their hand at folksinging.

He was getting a lot of input from different directions. Since he was singing in such a Guthriesque style, some people warned him that he was in danger of losing himself in Guthrie's shadow, to be dismissed as just a Guthrie imitator. "Guthrie was there in the thirties, these are the sixties, sing for now", they said.

He also discovered Lord Buckley, an old white comic, who was converse with the hip argot of black jazz and spoke wonderful, pointed monologues that cut into everything from women and jazz to the Nazz (the Nazarene) himself and the nature of good and evil.

Dylan transformed one of Buckley's renditions, *Black Cross*, about an over-educated "nigger" who was hanged by his ignorant white neighbors, into a talking blues number entitled *Hezekiah Jones*, in which he added some of his own flourishes.

On July 29, Dylan played at a hoot at the Riverside Church. A tape was made, of which some of it has appeared on bootleg records like *Early 60s Revisited*. He was nervous at first but did a creditable job of several songs including *Poor Lazarus* and *Handsome Molly (I Wish I Was In London)*. He also did harmonica accompaniment for Danny Kalb, a rising young blues guitarist from Wisconsin, on *Mean Ol' Southern Train*. At the end of the concert he came back to do an impromptu song with Jack Elliott, something called *Acne*, in which Elliott does loud doo-wahs and Dylan makes up lines about teenage anxiety like "Found out I had acne/Now you won't ask me/To the senior prom/Woo-oo..."

According to some accounts, it was also this concert that brought Bob and Suze Rotolo together. Suze, the girl pictured with Dylan on the cover of *Freewheeling Bob Dylan*, the second album, was described by contemporaries as "a Botticelli" woman, but she was a seventeen year-old with a very active mind, interested in art and very much a part of the Greenwich Village scene. She was seriously involved in the rising civil rights movement, she worked at CORE, helping out with the paper work, and knew just how frightening, how dangerous it was for the early freedom riders and black activists in the deep South.

Suze was out of school for the summer, while Bob had little in the way of work; soon they were inseperable. The relationship was intense, for in Suze, the young Dylan had found someone whom he felt he could trust, whom he could lean on for emotional support. In New York, the vista of the abyss was always there. Dylan knew he trod a very thin wire and that the only safety net was way back in Hibbing, Minnesota.

Now at parties they would be found together usually, isolated and absorbed in their own scene, often quite oblivious of the drinking and arguing going on around them.

Their friends noticed how quickly he became dependant on her, and some also felt that Suze, at seventeen, had taken on more than she realized. Her whole life still lay stretched out ahead, filled with mystery and the unknown; but her love affair with Dylan threatened to take over her life, and she was serious about her art. She intended to go to Italy soon to pursue that study.

Among other things that we can only speculate about Suze Rotolo is how much she influenced Dylan. Certainly she read the French Poets, Rimbaud, Verlaine, and hitherto Bob was largely unread. The Okie-ification he'd undergone had demanded the study of the guitar and country songs, songs of the people and the places they made. However it is also known that Dylan did reach out for all these sources, from Rimbaud to the civil rights struggle. Suze was constantly bringing back stories from CORE and Dylan was beginning to write songs about the oppression that was so rampant in the USA. He used almost anything as the spark for a song, for example *The Ballad Of Donald White* was triggered by a TV special on a "Volcano Named White", that focused on a convicted black felon awaiting execution.

In early August Bob went up to Boston once more, to check out Club 47 again. He wasn't getting much work in New York; it couldn't hurt. While there though, he met Carolyn Hester and her husband Richard Farina. Carolyn was one of the early big names in the Folk Music revival that was sweeping the campuses now. She had a couple of albums out, light, wholesome material that had commercial appeal. Carolyn herself was a fresh-faced blonde from Texas, and thus was a shoo-in for the cover photo on the Saturday Evening Post when they did a story on the Folk phenom.

They got along well and even spent a day on the beach together. On the beach Dylan, Ric von Schmidt and Richard Farina discussed music and performing. That night Carolyn was scheduled to appear at Club 47. After Richard had sung a song during her set, they made a point in inviting Dylan onto the stage to sing a few songs for the Cambridge folkies.

Carolyn Hester had been signed to Columbia Records earlier that year by John Hammond. For her first major label album, she was casting about for something unusual, perhaps something stronger in terms of material, than had been the case with her previous records. Some time during August she and Richard Farina decided to ask Dylan to "do something" on her record.

Bob got back to New York to find that he'd aroused some interest in other directions as well. He heard that Robert Shelton, folk music critic of the New York Times had been inquiring about him. Then there was a call from, of all people, Harry Belafonte and Hugo Montenegro who wanted a harmonica sound on the new Belafonte album they were making. Dylan, one of the most prominent youngsters playing harmonica, went into the studio to do back-up harmonica for Belafonte. Bob found the recording studio routine a crashing bore. In disgust he gave up on it after doing just a single track, the title cut from *Midnight Special,* and stomped home. "Over and over again" he groused, "who needs that. How many times can I play the same song over and over? The whole thing was overdone, a drag."

It seems clear that Dylan's famous disdain for lengthy recording sessions was there from the start.

In early September, Carolyn Hester asked him to record with her. At an early meeting to discuss what he might contribute, Dylan met John Hammond, the director of talent acquisition at Columbia Records.

> I saw this kid in a peaked hat playing not terribly good harmonica, but I was taken with him. I asked him, 'Can you sing? Do you write? Why don't you come up to the studio? I'd like to do a demo session with you, just to see how it is.

Hammond also felt a strong urge to sign Dylan. "I thought, I gotta talk contract right away" as there was this force in the kid; he was pale, skinny, often unkempt but people were struck by a tremendous force for music, a torrential enthusiasm that was inspiring, that could not be quenched.

However, before Hester could get Dylan on her record, or Hammond could get him into the studio for a demo, Dylan got on record again, playing harmonica with three aged but sprightly black musicians. Victoria Spivey, a star of the 1920s, who had written hundreds of songs in her career, was recording an album with three distinguished black musicians, Big Joe Williams, Roosevelt Sykes and Lonnie Johnson. The album, called *Three Kings And The Queen* has Bob Dylan playing bluesy, powerful harp behind Big Joe on *Sitting On Top Of The World*, *Wichita* and *It's Dangerous*. Dylan, by all accounts, did an excellent job in accompanying Big Joe, who was a solo artist renowned for his own unpredictable, difficult way of playing, which was very fast, rarely the same way twice. Victoria Spivey said of Bob: "He's a born genius of a musician."

Things were starting to happen; Dylan could feel it already. Nor was he the only one who kept an interested eye on the nascent folk scene. In New York there was Albert Grossman who had come up from managing The Gate of Horn jazz and folk club in Chicago to manage Odetta and then a hot new act called Peter Paul & Mary who were popularizing the folk revival and selling the results on a wider scale than anyone had dreamed possible. A plump man, nicknamed "the floating Buddha", he was regarded with some scorn by purists in the folk movement as the grand commercializer. Now he approached Dylan. Bob was cautious at first; he carefully checked Grossman out, asking the opinion of others like John Hammond. The picture he received, while not necessarily complimentary, was reassuring in many ways. Albert was devoted to success and that meant commercial success. He was fiercely protective of his artists as well and a tough negotiator of contracts. Dylan without signing anything, began to let Grossman do things for him, wanting to see what would result from having such an agent, someone who could exercise leverage on his behalf.

Almost immediately Mike Porco, on Grossman's advice, booked Dylan for another two-week stint at Gerde's. And over at the folklore center, Israel Young, who was soon to become embittered by the corruption of the folk scene by commercial success, wrote in his diary on October 13:

Grossman thinks Bob Dylan has a much better chance of making it. I just made an arrangement with Bob Dylan to do a concert in early November. Al Grossman spurred me to do it.

However, neither Dylan nor Grossman told anyone of their arrangement. It remained a secret for months.

Dylan opened at Gerde's on September 26, playing a supportive role to the top-billers, the Greenbriar Boys, but it was Dylan that got the great review, a couple of days later, from Robert Shelton, the Times' influential critic.

Shelton was very enthusiastic, calling Dylan in his review:

One of the most distinctive stylists to play in a Manhattan cabaret in months... there is no doubt that he is bursting at the seams with talent.

It was clear that as far as Shelton was concerned, Dylan was the best of the crop in Greenwich Village. He capped the review by declaring:

Mr. Dylan is vague about his antecedents and birthplace, but it matters less where he has been than where he is going, and that would seem to be straight up."

Needless to say, Bob was ecstatic; he raced around town with a copy of the piece in his pocket until it virtually disintegrated.

The review created some resentment in folk circles; Dylan was still the new kid in town and here he was already getting, in Jack Elliott's phrase, "a jet-propelled push" from the critics.

The review came out on the first day of Carolyn Hester's recording session and Bob took his copy with him and wound up showing everyone. Hammond saw it too and that was enough to get Hammond moving seriously in terms of getting Bob into the studio.

Dylan played harmonica on three songs on Hester's album, *Come Back Baby*, *Swing And Turn Jubilee* and *I'll Fly Away*.

In mid-October, he finally signed with Albert Grossman a full seven-year contract. At about the same time he went up to Columbia and cut some demos for Hammond. "He did *Talking New York* as the first one and when I heard him, I flipped", recalled Hammond. He told David Kapralik, head of A&R, that Dylan was going to be an important artist, "possibly not commercially", but in every other way. Kapralik discovered that Hammond was just ultra-enthusiastic about Dylan and thus found that he had "authorized the contract before even hearing Dylan."

Bob had been living on Avenue B in the East Village for a while; then he sojourned temporarily at Mikki Isaacson's place in Sheridan Square. Isaacson's place was a central social location for inner-folk crowd circles. Then Suze Rotolo's mother got an apartment in the same building and Dylan virtually moved into Mikki's space.

However, his contract with Columbia changed all that. He took an apartment on West 4th Street, just off Sixth Avenue. The rent was eighty dollars a month for a bachelor box, real Manhattan style; there was just enough room for him, his guitar, a fridge and a TV. He asked Suze to move in with him. She wouldn't; she was still under eighteen and not entirely certain that she wanted to live with Dylan. Their relationship remained idyllic; they were very happy but already she was troubled. She was concerned that her own ambitions were going to be submerged in what was happening to Bob. She sensed that something very powerful was beginning to take hold in him – he was writing all the time and his songs were getting better and better.

On November 4, Israel Young rented out the Carnegie Recital Hall, a small hall with the famous Carnegie Hall structure. Young had watched Dylan steadily grow during the year and had interviewed him for his journals. He explained: "I'm very excited by Bob Dylan. I'm producing a concert so I can hear him entirely."

In one of those interviews, Dylan pledged that:

> This concert isn't going to be a planned concert. I can
> offer songs that tell something of this America. No
> foreign songs. The songs of the land that aren't offered
> over TV or Radio and very few records.

The concert did not sell out. Possibly it was too far uptown for the younger section of the Village audience and Dylan was nervous and gave a rather jerky performance. Afterwards he apparently felt depressed; Izzy Young said later:

He did so many Jack Elliott things, using Elliott
mannerisms, using practically all Elliott material. Bobby
thought it was a failure.

A tape of this performance exists bearing songs like *Pretty
Peggy O, Gospel Flow, Fixin' To Die* and other standards of his
repertoire at this time. In addition, he did *1913 Massacre* to the
same tune as *Song To Woody*. (Clearly he'd taken Guthrie's
maxim about using any and every old tune you found as you
wished, to heart.)

The following week he went into the Columbia Studio and
cut his first album, *Bob Dylan*, in just four takes. It was short
and sweet, and angry.

There was a violent, angry emotion running through me
then. I just played the guitar and harmonica and sang
those songs and that was it. Mr. Hammond asked me if I
wanted to sing any of them over again and I said no. I
can't see myself singing the same song twice in a row.
That's terrible.

He recorded *Talking New York Blues* – his first, and rather
bitter song, dedicated to the great city. He cut *Song To Woody*
as well although, by now, he was no longer trekking out to the
hospital and back. In fact Marjorie Guthrie had won the battle
to have Woody transferred back to Brooklyn, near his home in
Howard Beach. The little weekends at the Gleason's came to
an end too. Dylan was beginning to try and put some distance
between himself and the Woody Guthrie legend. He told one
contemporary that he was "'going' far beyond Woody now."

Also on the album was a remarkable version of *House Of The
Rising Sun*, which Dylan borrowed from Dave Van Ronk. Van
Ronk was deeply hurt; he was due to record soon too and had
planned to use it. They didn't speak for months.

In mid-December he left Suze and the Village and went back
to Minnesota once more. Again his friends there were
impressed by the maturity that was visible and audible in him.
At some point during the visit he made a rather well-recorded
tape, the Minnesota Hotel Tape, which in whole or part has
appeared all over the world on bootlegs and even some 'official'
CBS albums, released in Italy.

The tape includes *Candy Man, Baby Please Don't Go, Stealin',
Poor Lazarus, Wade In The Water, Dink's Blues, Gospel Plow, Long
John, See That My Grave Is Kept Clean* and several VD songs,
twenty-six songs altogether, ending with *Hezekiah Jones*.
One reason this tape was featured on so many later bootlegs
was that Dylan made copies and gave them to friends. To

everyone he said excitably, "wait'll you hear my album!" and "John Hammond, he's the big producer you know, well hey he says I'm gonna be bigger than Presley. Bigger than Presley!"

He was riding the curve, could obviously feel the path opening up in front of him and his egotism was simple and pure; the dream he'd brought to Minneapolis and Dinkytown had matured to the point where it was almost actual, it was real, he was gonna make it.

When he got back to New York he found Suze Rotolo was ready to move in with him. The situation was complicated by the fact that her mother was less than pleased by the sudden appearance of a scruffy young man, a near penniless folksinger in the life of her lovely daughter. In addition, there was Carla Rotolo, a few years older and wiser than Suze, and she too spoke against the relationship. There was pressure on Suze to give up Dylan but she resisted it for the moment.

Too many things were happening, although from most accounts, it seems that things were happening internally. Their homelife was pretty straightforward, mostly sitting around watching TV. Sometimes they drank wine, sometimes they smoked pot – often Bob played guitar and sang.

Late at night he wrote furiously.

Almost every time Suze went over to CORE to help stuff envelopes, she picked up another story from the south and the struggle for civil rights. Dylan was getting these tales undiluted by the rather timid, polite reportage that was being given on national TV. The gap between official reality, that which could be reported to the nation, and what was happening in Mississippi certainly impressed itself on Dylan.

# CHAPTER FOUR

## Blowin' In The Wind

**D**ylan had been in the city for less than a year, but with an album coming out and with considerable critical appraise and fan interest already evident, two new groups became interested in him: The businessmen, and the journalists. The resulting contest of wills between Dylan and both groups was to provide an intriguing and frequently amusing counterpoint to the litany of stardom that was shortly to surround him.

At Columbia, the marketeers were still a little bemused. They didn't really know what to make of him. He just didn't fit their mould. To them "Folk Music" meant the Kingston Trio or Carolyn Hester. Pete Seeger was a "protest" figure and not someone that was really safe to be associated with. Seeger was still being hounded by the remnants of McCarthyism. Everyone was still very much afraid of that sort of thing.

Now they had this kid singing somewhat in the manner of Guthrie; a rural style, quick-witted, funny but crude. The songs were honest, honed sharp and direct from the heart and aimed at corpulent and corrupt targets like the (then) official acceptance of racism in the USA. This was just too wild for 1961. But marketing is a business for the quick and the sly and by now, the rumor that Al Grossman himself was managing Dylan, was beginning to spread. Ears pricked up at the news and so, despite the freakiness of the kid, they were drawn.

The Music Corporation of America (MCA), then just a very large talent agency, was interested from very early on. They talked to Grossman and Albert persuaded Bob to audition for some corporate types. He sang; they were baffled.

"They need more time to decide what you are", he was told.

There was even some brief interest from the Ed Sullivan show, which was the way to break an artist on the national scene; but it proved premature. So despite Grossman, Bob wasn't getting rich very quickly at this point. There wasn't all that much work to be had singing folksongs. However, there was one significant change from the previous year: He was writing his own songs now and they were rapidly improving.

By the end of January, he'd written the *Ballad Of Emmett Till*, which he told Israel Young was "the best thing I've ever written. Only song I play with a capo. Stole the melody from Len Chandler, a song he wrote about a Colorado bus driver."

Emmett Till concerned a black youth who'd been murdered in '55 during a visit to his uncle in Mississippi. Ostensibly, he was killed for whistling at a white woman. The killers were never convicted.

On February 12 came another new song, inspired by a TV documentary called A Volcano Named White, concerning a convicted killer. He borrowed the tune from folksinger Bonnie Dobson's version of *The Ballad Of Peter Amberley* and called it *Ballad Of Donald White*. Discussing the song Dylan said:

> I'd seen Donald White's name in a Seattle paper in about 1959. It said he was a killer. The next time I saw him was on a television set. My gal Suze said I'd be interested in him, so we went and watched. Donald White was sent from prisons and institutions 'cause they had no room. He asked to be sent back 'cause he couldn't find no room in life. He murdered someone 'cause he couldn't find no room in life. Now they killed him 'cause he couldn't find no room in life. They killed him and when they did I lost some of my room in life. When are people gonna wake up and see that sometimes people aren't really their enemies but their victims?

Obviously, Bob was ready to tackle a wide variety of oppressions; he wasn't going to restrict himself to simple questions.

The great Nuclear Fallout Shelter phenomenon also came in February. Responding to the new ICBMs that'd been developed to carry those H-bombs, Americans rushed to build fallout shelters in which to survive nuclear war. The futility of this nonsense – people walling off spaces in their basements against the power of multi-megaton weapons, plus all that radiation – moved Dylan to write a fine, ironic, but hopeful song called *Let Me Die In My Footsteps*, or alternately, *I Will Not Go Down Under The Ground*.

He wasn't alone in addressing these things; other folksingers were writing too. In fact, on both sides of the Atlantic there was a great surge of interest in topical folk-songs. In February, a small mimeographed publication appeared for the first time.

It was called Broadside and was devoted to publishing folk-songs, especially those that were written to protest the wrongs of society.

At the end of February the album, titled simply *Bob Dylan*, was released. It really was surprisingly good – Bob's top notch Guthrie set plus *Song To Woody* and *Talkin' New York Blues*. It got a reasonably good reception from critics. Folk music purists disliked it intensely – they had expected to. The small cadre of Dylan fans loved it, but Columbia soon discovered that there weren't all that many of them just yet; the record sold 4,200 copies on initial release.

Moreover, it was already a fossil. He was consciously moving away from the idolatry of Woody Guthrie that had obsessed him only a year before. He later told Nat Hentoff about the process of weaning himself away from that dependance on Guthrie:

> After I'd gotten to know him, I was going through some very bad changes, and I went to see Woody, like I'd go to somebody to confess to. But I couldn't confess to him. It was silly. I did go and talk with him, as much as he could talk, and the talking helped. But basically, he wasn't able to help me at all. I finally realized that. So Woody was my last idol.

He'd discovered that his hero was really just another human being. A great man, but one who was faithless to many women, who drank too much, and who never even acknowledged most of the children he'd fathered across the country during his career.

With copies of his album in hand, Bob went on another trip back to Minneapolis. There he impressed many old friends with a new found arrogance. He'd made it from the small pond of Dinkytown; he was on the first rung of the ladder to success and, back at the Ten 'O Clock Scholar, it felt good to let his old friends know it.

Once back in New York, John Hammond advised him to sign with a music publisher, both to get some advance money and also to protect copyright. He was sent to see Lou Levy of Leeds Music Publishing. Dylan made a demo tape, which has made it onto the Dylanophile market on a couple of bootleg albums (*Early 60s Revisited* and *Poems In Naked Wonder*). On this tape are songs like, *He Was A Friend Of Mine*, *Ramblin' Gamblin' Willie*, *Poor Boy Blues* and *Hard Times In New York* plus *Talkin' Bear Mountain Picnic Massacre Blues*. Bob signed with Leeds for five hundred dollars and his earliest songs were published on Leeds' subsidiary, Duchess Music.

In April, Bob's writing suddenly struck gold; he wrote his first big hit *Blowin' In The Wind*. The idea, he said, came after a long conversation about civil rights and the challenge to Americans to fulfill the dreams and promises of the constitution.

> The idea came to me that you were betrayed by your silence. Betrayed by the silence of the people in power. They refuse to look at what is happening. And the others, they ride the subways and read the Times, but they don't understand. They don't know. They don't even care – that's the worst of it.

In an interview with Sing Out!, Dylan said of the song:

> There ain't too much I can say about this song except that the answer is blowing in the wind. It ain't in no book or movie or TV show or discussion group. Man, hip people are telling me where the answer is but oh I won't believe that. I still say it's in the wind and, just like a restless piece of paper, it's got to come down some time. But the only trouble is that no one picks up the answer when it comes down, so not too many people get to see and know it… and then it flies away again.

The song excited a lot of people; it was taken up by the Civil Rights Movement, and it was immediately compared with such folk-standards as Pete Seeger's *If I Had A Hammer*, or any of Guthrie's greatest songs. It was published in Broadside at the end of May and soon became a favorite on the nation's campuses among young folksingers.

At about the same day it was published, Bob turned twenty-one. Also in May '62, Dylan did an interview show with Pete Seeger for WBAI Radio, in New York. He made his famous remark about the songs that were pouring out of him by this time:

> I don't sit around and write songs with the newspapers, like a lot of people do, spread newspapers around and pick something out to write a song about. It's usually right there in my head before I start. That's the way I write. But I don't consider it writing songs. When I've written it I don't even consider that I wrote it when I got done… I just figure that I made it up or I got it some place. The song was there before I came along. I just sort of came and just sort of took it down with a pencil, but it was all there before I came around. That's the way I feel about it.

For the show, which was never aired, he also did a couple

of songs, *Emmett Till* and *Donald White*. It's interesting to note that this rendering of *Donald White* is the only one to have survived and become widely available, albeit on bootlegs and tapes.

Why Dylan so self-consciously disowned his own creative powers like this is hard to understand, except that perhaps he felt a little awe at what was happening to him. All the material, all the songs and music that he'd absorbed, was reforming inside his head; now he was writing exciting songs that were just jumping off his ballpoint, night after night.

While his new songs were stunning to his contemporaries and even himself, there were clouds on the horizon in his relationship with Suze Rotolo. She had found an outlet for some of her energies in illustrating – to go with his songs in Broadside – and she was doing some painting. But her mother had invited her to take a trip to Italy that summer, to stay for several months and to study art.

Friends of theirs saw it as a classic tactic by Mrs Rotolo to prise her daughter away from the scruffy folksinger, whom she did not particularly like. Moreover, Suze was becoming more ambivalent about everything, as living with Bob was submerging her own personality in his career and she was feeling more and more trapped.

For a month she was torn. She asked friends what she should do. But in the end, on June 8, despite Bob's desperate entreaties to her to stay with him, she sailed for Italy with her mother.

By all accounts, her departure left Dylan distraught. He ceased to wash, or take care of himself. He seemed to be getting skinnier every day. People were worried about him, but his creative energies were, if anything, redoubled by his pain. More songs came like, *Don't Think Twice It's Alright* which he later described as "not a love song, it's a statement to make me feel better." Suze was to be gone for seven months.

From the summer of 1962, some interesting tapes have come down, spawning several varieties of bootleg records. One tape is the source of some confusion, being called by some, *The Gaslight Tape No.1* and by others, *The Canada Party Tape*. It appears in fact that much of the tape was made at the Finjan Club up in Montreal in June. Tracks from there include: *Blowin' In The Wind*, *Quit Your Lowdown Ways*, *Two Trains A Runnin'*, *Let Me Die In My Footsteps*, *Rocks And Gravel*, *He Was A Friend Of Mine*, *Stealin'*, *Emmett Till* and *Ramblin' On My Mind*.

Some months later Dylan was also taped while performing at the Gaslight, a famous Greenwich Village venue, and material from that performance was married to the Canadian tape. These tracks include newer songs like, *Don't Think Twice It's Alright*, *Hollis Brown* plus older items like *Hezekiah Jones* and *See That My Grave Is Kept Clean*.

Another tape from the same period is known as the *Gaslight Tape No.2*. This was probably recorded in July and has *Talkin' Bear* plus *Song To Woody*, *Pretty Polly* and *He Was A Friend Of Mine*. There is also a version of *Car Car*, in which Dylan is joined by Dave Van Ronk, who he introduces to the crowd as an "ex-blues singer" and which has been included on innumerable bootleg records since.

Also written in that summer were songs like *Tomorrow Is A Long Time*, *Down The Highway*, *Restless Farewell*, *Honey Just Allow Me One More Chance* and *Talkin' John Birch Society Blues*.

It's clear that while Suze's absence hurt him greatly, it also seems to have inspired him to write more and more new songs.

On August 9, he legally changed his name to Bob Dylan at Manhattan Supreme Court Building. Soon afterwards he heard from Suze that she wasn't coming back in September, that she intended to stay on in Italy and continue her studies. He was going to have to get along without her.

But things continued to bubble up; in September, Seventeen Magazine ran a big spread on Bob Dylan, with an interview he'd done back in the spring. He did some radio shows too and – remember this was 1962 – he soon rubbed some listeners the wrong way. On the Billy Faier show he did a spirited rendering of *Talkin' John Birch Society Blues*. An irate listener apparently then called in demanding that he should sing an anti-Communist song to go with his "pro-Communist" song. Dylan replied that he didn't happen to know any of those.

At the Carnegie Hall Hootenanny in September, he sang *Talkin' John Birch*, *Hollis Brown* and *Highway 61*. Dylan knew he had a good one in *Talkin' John Birch* which usually ignited an audience. The Folk music movement, already allied with the forces for social change, such as the Civil Rights movement, was inherently anti-war and friendly to the left. The John Birch Society had terrorized the left for years – a lot of people were ecstatic to see and hear the elfin figure of little Bobby Dylan get up there and demolish the Birchers to howls of laughter.

In October came the Cuban Missile Crisis and for a week or more the world trembled on the brink of nuclear war. Dylan's response was to write *A Hard Rain's A Gonna Fall*. This was to be his second big breakthrough song. Almost immediately Pete Seeger began to sing it. It spread rapidly via Broadside to the folksinger community. Dylan said of it:

> I wrote that when I didn't figure I'd have enough time left in life, didn't know how many other songs I could write during the Cuban thing. I wanted to get the most down that I knew about into one song, the most that I possibly could, and I wrote it like that. Every line in that actually is a complete song, could be used as a whole song. It's worth a song every line. Because I was a little worried.

Later in the same interview, he said:

> It's not atomic rain though. Some people think that. It's just hard rain, not the fallout rain, it isn't that at all. The hard rain that's gonna fall is in the last verse, where I say, 'the pellets of poison are flooding us all,' I mean the lies that people are told on their radios and in the newspapers trying to take people's brains away; all the lies I consider poison.

Hammond got Bob back into the studio at Columbia to begin work on the next album. In late November they recorded a single, *Mixed Up Confusion*, which had *Corrina Corrina* on the B side. It didn't work very well, and was quickly withdrawn when radio stations snubbed it. Dylan described it as "bright country rock" with piano and other instruments on it. John Hammond called it "a disaster".

Hammond was having to fight battles over Dylan on two fronts now. First, he was under siege at Columbia – a war party of old Columbia hands was said to be after Hammond's scalp. A demand was even sent up to drop Dylan's contract since the first album had sold in disappointing numbers. Some were even calling Bob 'Hammond's folly' behind his back.

Of Dylan's contract, Hammond said simply: "Over my dead body." Since Hammond had brought Goddard Lieberson, President of Columbia Records, to the company, and since he was also responsible for the excellence of Columbia's Jazz list, he turned out to be too well set on the ground to be shifted.

Moreover, Hammond had one other very valuable ally in the battle to keep Dylan – Johnny Cash. Although Cash had gone without real solid chart success for a couple of years, he was still a giant figure in the Country Music world. His support for Dylan was a solid gold recommendation. The Columbia scalp hunters retired in disarray and work continued on the new album, to be called *The Freewheelin' Bob Dylan*.

The other front was set up by Albert Grossman. Albert wanted Hammond's influence on Bob removed. He also wanted to try and break the Columbia contract and get Dylan into the open market where he was sure he could make Bob a lot more money quickly than would be the case with Columbia.

But the dismal failure of *Mixed Up Confusion* made December a pretty dismal month for Bob until, out of the blue, came an offer from the BBC. He was asked to play a couple of songs during a BBC TV Play in London, to be called Madhouse On Castle Street. They offered one thousand dollars and Bob accepted cheerfully and headed straight for Perugia, Italy, to track down Suze. Unfortunately he got there a couple of days too late, she was already on her way back to New York. While in Italy he continued to write great songs.

"I was in Italy with Odetta", he later told Anthony Scaduto. "Suze had gone back to the States and that's when I worked up the melodies of *Boots of Spanish Leather* and *Girl From The North Country."*

Soon he turned northwards and headed for London. Once there, he hooked up with Richard Farina (who'd left Carolyn Hester and Ric von Schmidt) who he'd met in Boston. Together they stayed in a hotel in South Kensington and roved out at night to the folk clubs and pubs. London had a healthy folk-music scene, centered on famous pubs where beer, hashish and folk-song went together in a fairly delirious brew. The three American folksingers played at some clubs, got outrageously loaded at others and even found time to record some songs in the basement studio of Dobell's Record Shop in the Charing Cross Road. Dylan did some harmonies with Farina and von Schmidt, under the guise of 'Blind Boy Grunt' on a few tracks.

On January 12 the play Madhouse On Castle Street was aired. It received less than favorable reviews, although Dylan was generally singled out for praise. "Interesting", said the Daily Mirror of the young "hobo guitarist."

A few days later, Bob flew back to New York and Suze Rotolo. They were together again, at last. And at first things went well, she returned to live with him on West 4th Street. In late January or early February she posed with him for the photograph session from which the cover for *Freewheelin'* arose.

He renewed work on the album. His new songs, the output of the year – he put Woody Guthrie behind him – were breaking new ground, opening up the files of the "tradition" of folk-song to a torrent of new ideas.

However, as the album progressed, so the interested parties around this emerging young star began to jostle for control and percentage points.

Al Grossman was unhappy with the deal that Dylan had got from Columbia. He itched to get Dylan out of a contract signed when Bob was under twenty-one. He had Peter, Paul & Mary under contract to Warners; he knew Dylan would attract an offer from any worthwhile record company now. But Hammond's deal proved to be solid. It seemed that Dylan had spent too much time in the Columbia studios since he'd turned twenty-one. The contract he'd signed as a minor had been cemented by his acceptance of studio time. Albert had to live with the contract, but he didn't feel he had to live with Hammond. He agitated for Hammond's removal from any role in the production of Dylan's records.

Hammond was ousted as producer and Tom Wilson, a young black producer working his way up the CBS ladder, was assigned to Dylan. Bob went back into the studio and cut *Girl From The North Country*, *Bob Dylan's Dream*, *Masters Of War* and *Talkin' World War III Blues*.

At about the same time, Dylan switched from Duchess Music to the Witmark publishing company. Warner Brothers was about to buy Witmark and Warner's chief Artie Mogull had heard all about Dylan, from Grossman, and others.

Dylan recorded a demo tape of forty-two songs for Witmark and created another important source of later bootleg records. The tape contains, among other things, a different version of *Talkin' John Birch Society* than the one most usually found on bootlegs. It also has several songs that were never put on official albums but might well have been, like *Seven Curses*, *Let Me Die In My Footsteps* and *Percy's Song*.

Between the work on *Freewheelin'* and the songs on the Witmark Demo tape, it's clear that Bob Dylan had really hit his stride. Within seven or eight months he'd written two dozen or more songs, of which two or three were already classics, songs that were popular all across the country. The promise that had shown itself in his talking blues, in *Blowin' In The Wind*, was being fulfilled in a masterful way, using folk music for pop music. But this pop music was *Oxford Town* as well as *Blowin' In The Wind*. The vision was both tightly focused and spread wide in anthems.

In April, he gave his first concert as a noted artist, at the Town Hall in New York. It was a great success and once again Robert Shelton gave him a wonderful review in the New York Times. He sang *Walls Of Redwing*, *Who Killed Davey Moore*, *With God On Our Side* and several other lengthy songs. The audience response was enthusiastic and this concert was taped and eventually spawned many bootlegs such as *Zimmerman*, *While The Establishment Burns*, *Help* and even an official album called *More Bob Dylan Greatest Hits* which has *Tomorrow Is A Long Time* from this tape on it. Dylan sounds a little nervous throughout the show but the audience was solidly behind him, despite some overlong, even monotonous efforts. He ended the set with a poem called *Last Thoughts On Woody Guthrie*, in which he recalled the railroad tracks of Hibbing, his search for himself and for some sort of significance in life. He laid his identification with Guthrie to rest – He'd moved on now, that chapter was ended.

# CHAPTER FIVE

## Freewheelin'

**W**ith *Freewheelin'* finished, Al Grossman wanted to get Dylan as much exposure as possible. He called Howard Alk, owner of a club called The Bear in Chicago and though Alk wouldn't proffer any money, he did agree to let Dylan play there a couple of nights. Grossman had already been to see Studs Terkel, an American writer with a radio show in Chicago, and arranged an interview for Bob.

The interview went well and a tape of it exists which has been bootlegged too, although not extensively. Mr Terkel was somewhat stern and inquisitorial but Bob did his best to be nice and helpful, having not yet developed his interview 'armor'. He sang several songs including: *Blowin' In The Wind*, *Boots Of Spanish Leather* and *Hard Rain's A Gonna Fall*. Before singing this last number, Bob urged instead that Terkel play the record and explained that the "Hard Rain" that's gonna fall is not meant to be atomic rain or fallout, but just the general crack of doom that Dylan had felt coming so strong in the previous October.

At The Bear, Dylan met another rising young musician, albeit one in a specialist field, Mike Bloomfield, electric blues guitarist. Bloomfield had some vague intention of taking his guitar down to the club to indulge in the honored Chicago tradition and to get on stage during Dylan's performance to plug in and jam. Except that the jam would be to 'cut' Dylan, just blow away his performance and replace it with hard, driving electric blues. However, Bloomfield recalled to Ratso Slocum many years later:

> Me and my old lady were just bowled over watching him perform... this cat sang this song called *Redwing*, about a boy's prison and some funny talking blues about a picnic and he was fucking fantastic, not that it was the greatest playing or singing in the world, I don't know what he had man, but I'm tellin you I just loved it. I mean I could've watched it non-stop forever and ever.

60

Afterwards, Bloomfield met Bob and they hit it off well together. This friendship was to serve Dylan well in the future.

Back in New York, Albert had exciting news: The Ed Sullivan Show was definitely interested in Bob Dylan. *Blowin' In The Wind* was everywhere now. Bob went to audition for Sullivan and Bob Precht, the producer of the show. He sang *Talkin' John Birch Society Blues*. They loved him, certain that they had something that was not only controversial but funny, a kid with enough charisma to wake up the whole nation. And that, of course, was exactly what the Sullivan show was meant to do on its Sunday night slot.

Furthermore, they knew that Dylan's songs were really stirring something big up on the folk scene. Peter, Paul & Mary, Grossman's other major act, had hit the singles charts in March with *Puff The Magic Dragon*, a piece of nonsense that had reached No. 2 for a couple of weeks. At every performance – Peter, Paul & Mary were constantly performing – they sang *Blowin' In The Wind* after introducing it with the words... "And now we'd like to sing a song written by America's most important young writer..."

However, on the weekend of the show itself, when the men upstairs at Columbia discussed *Talkin' John Birch Society Blues* with the legal staff, there was a strange panic. Stowe Phelps, editor of program practises, was dispatched on Sunday afternoon, just hours before the show, to say that the song could not be used. Dylan was furious, he left the studio and went home, and did not appear on the Sullivan show that night.

Sullivan later told a TV columnist, Bob Williams:

> We fought for the song. We pointed out that President
> Kennedy and his family are kidded constantly by TV
> comedians. Governor Rockefeller is also kidded, among
> others. But the John Birch Society – I said I couldn't
> understand why they were being given such protection.
> But the network turned us down. They understood and
> sympathized with our viewpoint but insisted they had
> previously handled the Birch Society, and their lunatic
> behaviour on network news progress, and couldn't take
> the subject into entertainment.

Soon afterwards the corporate enforcers were in the offices of Columbia Records demanding that *Talkin' John Birch Society Blues* be yanked off the *Freewheelin'* album. Once again, Dylan was enraged at this attempt to censor him. He swore to friends that he'd record with that song or not record at all.

The crunch came quickly, and it was apparent that it was just too early in the game for Bob and Al Grossman to win this one. Everything was stacked against them. The first album had not been a sales success. Hammond had had to go to the mattresses to save Dylan's contract for the second record. Now Hammond was somewhat alienated by Grossman's maneuvers. The record company, moreover, had a lot of material already recorded. They could release some kind of album anyway, whether Bob liked it or not.

Dylan had to re-think. Putting out the record was the most important thing, beside that fact everything else paled into insignificance. And while looking at it again, he changed his mind about other tracks. He removed more of the Guthrie influence, possibly more evidence, if it's needed, of how quickly he was changing through this period – what may have been good enough in December was not good enough in May. *Talkin' John Birch* came off along with *Rocks & Gravel, Ramblin' Gamblin' Willie, Let Me Die In My Footsteps*. In their place he put *Girl From The North Country, Masters Of War, Bob Dylan's Dream* and *Talkin' World War III Blues*.

This switch came at the last minute when Columbia had already released a few hundred copies of the original record, thus inaugurating the now colossal market for Dylan memorabilia.

Bob was disgusted, and naturally there were critics and even friends who attacked him for giving in to CBS. He disappeared to Al Grossman's house at Woodstock for a while. When he reappeared, he did his best to shrug it off. "Who needs it?" he said, he had a career to build and this just wasn't the moment to be battling the record company.

Meanwhile, things with Suze Rotolo were slipping back to their old level. She was suppressed she felt, oppressed by Bobby's fame. Yet she was still contributing, doing nice line drawings for his songs in Broadside Magazine. And, of course, she still gave him emotional support, but friends noticed that she was increasingly becoming an outlet for him from the tension and pressure that was coming from every direction. She grew depressed as the months wore on. Back in January when the cover shot photo was taken, out on West 4th Street near the apartment, things had been rosy again, like the first days of their relationship back in '61. The glow faded, the fits and storms and tears returned, and began to destroy her. "He won't let me do anything", she complained to friends. But she knew that he needed her more than ever, because as *Freewheelin'* came out, Bob began to discover that there was a price to be paid for his new found fame.

*Freewheelin'* was a critical and a sales success. Dylan had a real income at last. In June, Playboy Magazine ran a piece on Folk Music and Nat Hentoff, the author, gave Dylan a lot of space. Hentoff called Dylan, "a penetratingly individual singer." Already, in late May, Time Magazine had had a shot at him with a piece called: "Let Us Now Praise Little Men", which tried to ridicule him.

Dylan was asked to appear at the Monterey Folk Festival at the end of May. There he met Joan Baez once more, but this time it was a Joan Baez that had actually listened to his songs. Her manager, Emanuel Greenhill, had given her an acetate of Dylan's songs that he'd been given by Grossman. She'd been struck by "the genius" she heard emerging in those songs.

At Monterey, his performance went down very well. But West Coast audiences were not yet as avid at bootlegging as those in the East, for no tape of this show has materialized.

After the festival he went down to Carmel and stayed with Joan Baez in her house for a week or more. It seems clear that they were already lovers.

Joan asked Bob to be her unannounced guest on stage during her next concert tour later that summer – a move that she knew would bring him much wider exposure, more quickly, than he could hope to get any other way.

In Carmel, she heard dozens of Dylan songs and sang them with him and by herself, picking through things for songs to sing herself or even to record. And while they were there, Peter, Paul & Mary released their cover of *Blowin' In The Wind* as a single. It immediately took off up the hit parade. Dylan listened in awe as the disc made three hundred thousand sales, becoming the fastest selling single in Warner Brothers' history. He was a national property now, a household name wherever households had college kids and teenagers. *Blowin' In The Wind* reached No. 2 in the singles charts, lingered there for a couple of weeks, and in all, spent fifteen weeks, right through the summer, in the best-sellers league.

Bob got back to New York in late June. It was obvious that things were going wrong with Suze, but there was a little time to try and mend them. Bob was invited to appear at a Civil Rights rally in Greenwood, Mississippi, on July 6. As the best known young protest songwriter who had written *the* anthem for the movement, it was imperative that he appeared.

The rally was held in the back yard of a black-owned farm, a few miles south of Greenwood. Three hundred rather brave individuals turned up to hear Pete Seeger, Theodore Bikel and "Bobby Dillon", as the New York Times called him, plus a black singing trio called the "Freedom Singers", from Albany, Georgia.

All day and night, during the rally, there were cars filled with white men parked in a row on the far side of the road. Other cars cruised up and down slowly. A police car was parked on the near side. With national newsmedia present, the local authorities were taking no chances.

Dylan sang a new song, *Only A Pawn In Their Game* or *The Ballad Of Medgar Evers*. The song was dedicated to Evers, a black field secretary for the NAACP who had been gunned down in June, in Jackson, Mississippi. The man indicted for the shooting came from Greenwood.

The biggest event of the summer however was set for the north, at the Newport Folk Festival. For several years the Newport festivals had been getting bigger and better and the 1963 festival was one of those great collective moments that, in some ways, describe the rise and fall of the so-called sixtie's spirit just by their recital; Newport '63, Woodstock, Altamont...

Fifty thousand folk fans were on hand for a full three days of music. Most of the crowd were students – many carried their own guitars – and everyone was singing Bob Dylan songs. His name was cheered continually throughout the day, long before his own performance.

When Peter, Paul & Mary came on and ripped into *Blowin' In The Wind*, a great roar went up and the entire audience sang along.

When Dylan himself finally appeared, it was to a huge ovation. Only that for the Queen of Folk, Baez herself, had been greater. Bob sang *Ye Playboys & Playgirls* with Pete Seeger and then began *Blowin' In The Wind*, which inspired Baez to come back on and sing it with him. Then they were joined by Seeger, the Freedom Singers and others and all sang *Blowin' In The Wind* while the crowd roared approval. The finale came with all the performers holding hands, swaying together while they sang *We Shall Overcome*. Afterwards Dylan said of the festival: "The crowd was fantastic, just fantastic."

However, Newport also revealed for Bob the new limitations to his life imposed by fame. He reacted in the ways that he was to become infamous for, with paranoia and an almost bizarre arrogance.

At one point, while out strolling the site, he and Dave Van Ronk were spotted and pursued by a horde of fans. They ran for a station wagon in which they made their escape. Dylan told Van Ronk, "get used to it Dave, next year it'll be you" and Van Ronk thought Dylan looked "terrified". Dylan did behave as if terrified by the audience reaction he'd aroused. However Joan Baez, who came to know the performer Bob Dylan as well as anybody else ever has, saw Dylan react to the same fan pressure with an ambivalence that he tried to suppress. Yet it was terrifying to be chased by a mob of girls, but it was sort of exciting as well.

However, to Dylan, the audience he'd wooed so well now turned into a "mob", a monster that reached for him remorselessly with endless tentacles. Once brought to life, though there was no way to turn the damn thing off, the beast had a perverse life of its own.

Backstage at the festival, protected from the "mob", Dylan was seen strutting about with a bullwhip, cracking it in the air, and snarling one line backhanders at anyone who bored him for an instant. This sort of thing upset a segment of the folk music establishment – their earlier fears about Dylan seemed confirmed. As folk was popularized, so it was corrupted; it turned into "protest" and now "pop" with hordes of fans and egotistical young performer stars. The old hands were distressed, even enraged by this.

Also observed at Newport was Suze Rotolo, looking wan and perhaps rather sad. She saw Dylan and Baez together, saw what was going on between them, and although amazed that Bob could actually do this, she accepted what was happening as gracefully as possible.

Joan's summer tour was starting up; the first date was August 3, right after the festival, in New Jersey. Bob would appear with her for the second half of her set.

He continued to appear alongside Joan, in what became a memorable series of concerts, one of the high points of the Folk Music boom.

By the third week of August though, while Bob Dylan was treading firmly upwards to a fame set in the concrete of myth, morticed with solid record sales, Suze was gone. She left the 4th Street apartment and went to live with her mother in New Jersey.

It seems that Bob couldn't handle the apartment without Suze, because he now spent a lot of time at Albert Grossman's big house in Bearsville, near Woodstock. Woodstock, set in the Catskill Mountains one hundred and fifty miles north of New York City, was an artist's colony founded in 1910 and inhabited at that time by painters, potters, poets and writers. It was peaceful and Bob and Joan could hang out in the bars and coffee houses without drawing a mob scene of autograph hunters and the like.

On August 28, he went down to Washington DC for the great Civil Rights March and, while there, he was introduced to the vast crowd and sang *Only A Pawn In Their Game*. A fragment of the song was recorded, before a loud-voiced gentleman began orating right over Bobby's singing. The fragment has appeared on several bootlegs and on an official album called *We Shall Overcome*, a various artistes compilation put out by Folkways Records.

In September he split his time between staying at Woodstock and writing new songs and went down to New York to record them in the studio. The next album took shape quickly. It was called *The Times They Are A Changing* and it constituted Dylan's most direct "protest" songs, such as *Only A Pawn In Their Game*, *With God On Our Side* and *The Times They Are A Changing* itself.

Other aspects of his developing songwriting talent were also on display in *Boots Of Spanish Leather*, *Restless Farewell* and *One Too Many Mornings*, the sad love songs – inspired in part by Suze Rotolo. There was also the stark tragedy of *Hollis Brown*. Dylan himself was most fond of *The Lonesome Death Of Hattie Carol*.

When Suze Rotolo moved back into the city in late September, she stayed at her sister's place on Avenue B, on the Lower East Side. Dylan soon showed up at the apartment and refused to leave. He moved in and refused to go. He even refused to let Carla Rotolo swap apartments with him and let her live in his place on West 4th street. There was no privacy in the little Avenue B place. The emotional tides were soon running high; the arguments were bitter.

And now the media were closing in, getting a clearer picture of him as a phenomenon, the rebel spokesman for a rebellious generation. They were sharpening knives on their typewriters.

But even as they closed in on the quarry, the 'real' Dylan was changing, rapidly. Some of the changes were due to plain old growing up. Some of the changes were from the powerful new drugs that were available. Dylan had used grass for years – marijuana had been part of the folk music scene since the late fifties. But more recently, the psychedelics, in particular LSD, had become available in Manhattan, and in California. This LSD was both legal and very strong, mostly made by Sandoz Pharmaceuticals Company. LSD only became illegal in 1966. In the American naturistic bohemia, framed by jazz-loving poets gone mad on wine and existence, that was allied to the Folk Music phenomenon at various levels, there was a sort of mounting uproar going on over LSD.

At Harvard University, Tim Leary and Richard Alpert were engaged in their soon-to-be-famous LSD experiments.

Dylan found the experience stimulating, opening up interesting connections. The progress towards expressing the inner, poetic vision that he'd been making before, accelerated; now he raced down new pathways. His songs changed dramatically and his intent foreshortened politically while intensifying on the personal level. No more 'anthems' of such obvious natures as *The Times They Are A Changing*, no more of what he called "finger-pointing songs."

To those with psychedelic eyes, the old politicos and folkies began to seem a little quaint, even antique.

This is not to say that Bob would turn his back on folk-song intrinsically, just on the Folk "movement" that had helped bring him to prominence. Since he'd turned to folk as a frustrated young rock'n'roller back in Hibbing, Bob had been dealing daily with visionary myth. In the great vault of folk-song, which serves as a collective repository of the bitter myths, wry memories and grim traditions of the anglo-saxon-dominated culture of the USA, Britain and Canada, Dylan found a lot of inspiration. Most of all he found that things were never simple.

Of Folk music he said: "It's never been simple", in an extensive interview with Nora Ephron and Susan Edmiston.

> It's weird man, full of legend, myth, Bible and ghosts. I've never written anything hard to understand, not in my head anyway, and nothing as far out as some of the old songs. They were out of sight. For example? *Little Brown Dog*… I bought a little brown dog, its face is all grey. Now I'm going to Turkey flying on my bottle. And *Nottemun Town*, that's like a herd of ghosts passing through on their way to Tangiers. *Lord Edward, Barbara Allen*, they're full of myth.

"And contradictions?" asked Nora and Susan.

"Yeah, contradictions" said Dylan. Contradictions abounded.

As soon as the album was in the can, Bob left Avenue B and flew west to appear with Joan Baez at the Hollywood Bowl. At this concert there appeared a small, but vocal minority, who howled their displeasure at the sight of Dylan. The comfortable world of Folk Music was being turned upside down now and to some he was the one responsible.

Contradictions everywhere, *The Times They A Changing* was another critical and sales success, the epitome of the "protest" album. But already he was way past "protest"; he was writing another kind of song, like *Lay Down Your Weary Tune*, which he unveiled at his next big concert, at Carnegie Hall in New York, in mid-October.

His parents were there; he flew them in especially to show them how their prodigal son had turned out. And, fortunately, the concert was a big success with no booing minority on hand. But then this was a Bob Dylan concert, not a Baez one. Besides old favorites like *John Brown* and *Davey Moore*, he performed *Dusty Old Fairgrounds* – a 'route' song of the carnivals and circus circuits – and *Lay Down Your Weary Tune*. A tape from this concert has passed onto many bootlegs like *Great White Wonder 2* and *Seems Like A Freeze Out*.

He ended the set with a poem called *Last Thoughts On Woody Guthrie*, in which he hurriedly recalled the railroad tracks of Hibbing and his search for himself and for some sort of significance in his life. He intended to lay his identification with Guthrie to rest for once and for all.

He may also have laid to rest Columbia's plans to record and release an album of the show because they felt that the eight-minute poem was just too uncommercial. In part, this explains the good quality of the many bootlegs that resulted from this tape and the acetates made from it.

The day after this success, Newsweek magazine hit the stands with a painful exposé of Bob Zimmerman. Dylan's middle-class roots were laid bare. But the piece went on from simple exposé; the knives were in too. Newsweek even went so far as to repeat a rumor, known to be false, that Bob hadn't written *Blowin' In The Wind* at all but had bought the song from a student in New Jersey.

Dylan was shocked, "Man they're out to kill me," he exclaimed to friends, "What've they got against me?" he wondered.

Clearly, Bob had underestimated the depth of the resistance to change in the USA. Even in the journalistic establishment there was a definite antipathy to the Civil Rights Movement, toward "liberal" notions.

The contradictions continued. When he was in New York he stayed with Suze. When he left town it was to go to Woodstock. It is said that Al Grossman played a vital role at this time in keeping Bob sane and stable. Grossman could help him plot out a course for his future, show him the results of working this way, seeking commercial success. Only the commercially successful would be sure of having artistic control of their product. Grossman also advised him about his diet, or the law, or almost anything. Dylan apparently told some friends that he never would have made it through '63 without Grossman to turn to.

In November, in the midst of planning for a small tour – a half dozen or so gigs in the western and southern states – there came the bombshell of President Kennedy's assassination. It stunned America, rocked the world and shook Bob Dylan quite a bit. His paranoia accelerated, because after all, he was articulating the kinds of demands that JFK had come to represent in the minds of many Americans who resented the law. Demands that America should cease to be an apartheid society, that it should allow the black minority full political rights, which were still effectively denied in the south. As a whole, the nation saw the assassination of its President as a blow against change, although the murky reality behind the killing, behind Oswald, Jack Ruby, and everything that happened in Dallas that day, never became clear through the smoke that so swiftly enveloped it. Dylan however, had no trouble visualizing some angry person identifying him as the cause of hatred changes and taking a gun to a concert.

A couple of weeks after the assassination, Bob was awarded the Tom Paine Award of the Emergency Civil Liberties Committee for his work towards the Civil Rights campaign. His acceptance speech was a disaster. He'd been to Mississippi. He knew the streets and the dirty and mean life therein; he saw the well-heeled liberals at the tables in the Hotel Americana in New York and he wanted to vomit on the intellectuals. He said he didn't know anybody "that needs to wear a suit", he tried to say that Oswald had done something that everyone wants to do sometimes, (shoot a powerful person for some private reason), and that set the crowd to booing him. He insulted them – the middle-aged, the fur coats, the suits – and they got angry. Before he finished, Dylan claimed afterwards the chairman of the meeting was kicking him under the table.

After this fiasco, Dylan vowed to avoid any public involvement with any political causes. He decided to concentrate on songs and began to get ready for a cruise across America in the new year, driving to the gigs he had lined up for concerts in February.

Then in December '63, he began to be aware of a new phenomenon. At first it was just on the radio. New York deejays were going wild over a British group called The Beatles. Requests for Beatles' records were coming in strong although, at this point, the Beatles were only really known in Britain where they had been topping the charts solidly for a year and where Beatlemania was a sort of national crisis.

On December 30, the Beatles released their first American single *I Want To Hold Your Hand*, which was already a number one hit in Britain. On January 3, 1964, the Liverpool rockers appeared on the Jack Parr TV show and the madness began. Within three weeks *I Want To Hold Your Hand* had sold a million copies and plans to release five more Beatles' singles were being rushed through at Capitol Records. A newform of youthquake was underway and Dylan had an eye on it.

In fact, legend has it that during that first visit to America, in New York, the Beatles were introduced to Bob Dylan by Al Aronowitz, a journalist. Bob took along some grass to their hotel room, which was under total siege by fans, and turned them onto marijuana for the first time. He later told Anthony Scaduto:

> I had heard the Beatles in New York when they first hit...
> They were doing things nobody was doing. Their chords
> were outrageous, just outrageous, and their harmonies
> made it all valid. You could only do that with other
> musicians. Even if you're playing your own chords you
> had to have other people playing with you. That was
> obvious and it started me thinking about other people.

By the time Bob set out for his planned cruise of the nation on February 2, the Beatles had five singles in the top ten, all of them rapidly becoming gold records; there had been nothing like this since the days when Elvis Presley had first struck it big.

# CHAPTER SIX

# The Times They Are A-Changin'

It was 1964 and Bob Dylan was America's Crown Prince of Folk. The Folk Music movement was at its zenith and *The Times They Are A-Changin'* was a hot party record on campuses from Harvard to Berkeley. Bob however was profoundly restless, he was telling friends "I want to go out and feel what the people are feeling, find out what's goin' on."

It was as if he'd been caught in a Folk Music capsule, getting too specialized, too distant from popular taste. "There's more to music than protest, ever heard of fun?"

On February 2, he set out on his planned nationwide cruise. He had a Ford station wagon and several gigs scattered across the land over the ensuing month. Definite places to visit included New Orleans at Mardis Gras and Carmel, California – Joan Baez's home. On the way, at various post offices, he had a marijuana mailing system set up so the Ford's occupants could be refuelled every so often. In the car he had Victor Maimudes as driver-cum-bodyguard, Paul Clayton, a folksinger friend, and Pete Karman, a journalist on the New York Mirror and a friend of Carla Rotolo. He also had some used clothing he wanted to donate to striking miners in Hazard, Kentucky, plus his guitar and the typewriter.

They drove south into Virginia, stayed at Clayton's house and visited Carl Sandberg, a noted American poet – wove their way on into Kentucky and saw the miners. Then it was on further south, into Georgia. Bob gave a concert at Emory University, a black college. They sped on, into the heartland of Dixie, to Tougaloo College, another black school, this time in Mississippi. Police cruisers of course followed them from time to time – Police were sure to tail any car with orange New York state license plates. There was enough grass in the car to get them all one hundred years and what might've happened if Bob Dylan had been busted for marijuana in Mississippi at this time, only a couple of months after the Kennedy assassination and with harsh anti-marijuana laws everywhere, is something that must've had Albert Grossman shuddering in his sleep.

But they made it down to New Orleans for Mardis Gras. Fat Tuesday in the great swamp city, Queen of the Mississippi, and a scene of spectacular lunacy during the week of revels. Apart from getting thrown out of a black bar, Dylan and entourage seemed to have stayed high and mobile and had a generally great time of it.

They roamed on into the west. Stopped in Dallas to check out Dealey Plaza and the Book Depository building for themselves. Drove on across the great flatness of west Texas, into Colorado and the mountains.

Eventually they reached San Francisco in time for Dylan's gig at Berkeley Community Theatre. This was an important concert for him, his first on his own in California. It drew kids from all over the West Coast. In the second half he introduced Joan Baez as *his* unannounced guest. He did the songs from the last two albums for the most part, but no tape of this concert has surfaced on bootlegs yet. However it became for California one of those great collective moments of consciousness moulding, like Newport '63 had been, that was talked about for months, for years.

At a party in Berkeley Dylan met up with Bob Neuwirth, who was to become an important person in the group around Dylan over the next two years. Neuwirth was also a folksinger, and he'd been singing professionally for a couple of years longer than Dylan. He had a caustic wit and a cynical sense of humor that dovetailed with Dylan's own.

After the Berkeley concert, Karman the journalist was bumped from the Ford and Neuwirth took his place. They drove down to visit with Joan at Carmel. It was an intriguing moment. In the beautiful valley of Carmel, with Joan's mother, visiting her from Paris, making a beef stew in the house, they sat out and drank wine together. Bob and Joan, surrounded by his travelling entourage of "mindguards", folksingers, travellers, and they were the King and Queen of Folk, or Pop-Folk at least. The age beckoned them urgently. The times were in fact changing; a chasm of war was opening in Vietnam as well.

Joan was to record some Dylan songs on her next album. They made plans to continue appearing together.

When Bob finally got back to New York, and to Suze Rotolo, there were more ugly scenes. He couldn't let Suze alone but neither could he resolve the contradiction posed by his affair with Joan Baez. Suze had had quite enough. She left in March forever, going back to New Jersey to live with her mother. This proved to be the end of their relationship. Despite Dylan's entreaties, Suze never came back.

Of the pain and the viciousness, the bitter tides in that little apartment, Bob left an indelible memento in the *Ballad Of Plain D*, which he wrote soon afterwards.

He was soon caught up in the progress of his career again. A concert tour of England was arranged and beforehand he stayed in Woodstock, at Grossman's place. Eventually he gave up the apartment on West 4th street and so, when in town, he stayed with friends.

There were lots of new songs churning in his mind now and they were just as radical a shift from what had gone before as *Ballad In Plain D* was from *Boots Of Spanish Leather*.

To friends like Phil Ochs, he announced brusquely:

The stuff you're writing is bullshit because politics is bullshit. It's all unreal. The only thing that's real is inside you. Your feelings, the world is, well it's just absurd.

Dylan had cultivated the poet's detachment from the culture. He'd spent some time researching the roots of madness, the chasms separating people from one another; he'd examined himself too, on drugs, in cars, in pool halls and bus stations. He'd even been across the country by automobile – he was primed with impressions and ideas. He'd reached the conclusion that many other young radical thinkers were reaching at the same time. "Protest" was considered dumb, that trying to alter the way the world operated would take more than just a rearrangement of the national politics via the ballot box. His impatience with the rate of change, the youthful insistence on clarity and purpose, was now tinged with the cynicism of his later vision. There was a "truer" poet's purpose building up in him now.

In May the tour of England went very well, complimented by good crowds in most of the cities he visited. He met the Beatles again, spent time with them and as he told an interviewer later, had a great time, "we just laughed all night." This was the infancy of the psychedelic era, London was "swinging" at night, and the Beatles and the other young Rockocrats, like Brian Jones, were happy drunkards, often to be seen "looning" in clubs like the Scotch of St. James, Annabel's and the rest.

Dylan saw that the British groups – from the Beatles to the Animals, or the Kinks, the Yardbirds, Rolling Stones, Manfred

Mann – were all revitalizing rock 'n' roll. Rock was coming back to life with a vengeance and considering Bob's past, he must have had a strong inclination to go in the rock direction himself. And yet he had this large audience to whom he was a "folksinger", and to whom rock 'n' roll was anathema.

After the tour, he wandered down through Europe to Greece where he stayed for a while, relaxing and writing up the songs he'd been developing for the next album. Once back in New York in June, he went into the studio for an historic recording session.

*Historic* perfectly describes this event, which was recorded for Posterity by Nat Hentoff, writing a profile of Dylan for the New Yorker magazine. Tom Wilson was the producer and Dylan brought some friends along, plenty of Beaujolais, seven completed songs and six fragmentary ones.

Eleven songs made it onto the album. Eight or nine others, out-takes from *Another Side Of Bob Dylan* sessions have surfaced on such bootlegs as *Great White Wonder, Stealin', Seems Like A Freeze Out* etc. These tracks were *New Orleans Rag, Denise Denise, I'll Keep It With Mine, That's Alright Mama, East Laredo, Lay Down Your Weary Tune* and *California*.

It has been claimed by Rolling Stone magazine that *I'll Keep It With Mine* was written for Nico, who was soon to sing with the Velvet Underground. Nico had suddenly appeared on the New York scene after a modelling career in Germany. Perhaps this explains why Dylan didn't choose to include such a fine song on this album.

Songs he performed included, like *Chimes Of Freedom*, image-crowded sung poems, filled with things like "hypnotic splattered mists" and without a single "protest" in the bunch.

At the 1964 Newport Folk Festival, Bob Dylan was an accomplished star; he bestrode the affair like a colossus. You were either a fan or you hated him and what he'd "done to Folk." He turned away from protest entirely, instead he sang the songs of *Another Side Of Bob Dylan*. The audience was amazed. The younger elements on the whole went with Dylan. The older heads, those who were closer to the traditional folk movement, didn't approve. Cries of shock and pain were to be heard from the likes of Irwin Silber, the editor of the folk music journal Sing Out!

Bob's only reply was to sing *I Shall Be Free No.10* and demonstrate once again his mastery of the humor in the situation. The funny talking blues style he'd once relied on had been honed down now to a single strand in his set, but he'd refined it to a rapier.

Another input that summer came from Allen Ginsberg who met Bob through Al Aronowitz, a figure who appears repeatedly in the story of sixties rock culture, where he performed the essential function of introducing famous, heavily guarded people to each other. Ginsberg had turned his personal search for enlightenment into a gentleman's crusade to spread karmic peace and quiet on the embroiled world's waters. Allen became an enthusiast and a good influence, at least poetry-wise. Dylan was now reaching out for new reading – Allen had read it all.

In August *Another Side Of Bob Dylan* was released, to heavy initial sales. The cries of "sellout" were raised anew. Bob began to grow somewhat weary and bitter about the "Folk Music Movement."

"They" – a collective noun for traditional-minded artistes, publishers, club owners, fans and record collectors – charged that they'd been used; that this clever middle class kid had come in and played on their sympathies; that they had not only given him a boost but they'd made his career, and now when he'd caught the imaginations of the young generation of the sixties, he was cashing in and copping out of the struggle.

Perhaps they were hurt so badly because they'd seen him as their ultimate riposte to McCarthyism. Bob Dylan was going to take back the minds of Americans from the right wing and deliver up the pop charts and the campuses to the left wing intelligentsia that had survived on the outer margins for so long.

Except that here, he'd matured and started to write songs about himself. This, to them, was unacceptably self-indulgent. He was their folksinger idol -- he wasn't supposed to mutate into a pop star. Besides, he was just a kid, and they – with their literary backgrounds complete – were too remote to understand what it was to be twenty-three years old, torn between two powerful love affairs.

Speaking about *Another Side*, Dylan was to comment in 1966:

> The songs are insanely honest, not meanin' to twist any heads and written only for the reason that I, myself, me alone wanted and needed to write them. I've conceded the fact, there is no understanding of anything, at best just winks of the eye and that's what I'm looking for now I guess.

Through the summer he continued to move between Woodstock and New York, breaking to do concerts here and there, and basically writing all the time. He had a contract for a book entitled *Tarantula*, and the songs kept tumbling out –

great songs. In August he penned *Mr. Tambourine Man*; soon afterwards he wrote *It's Alright Ma (I'm Only Bleeding)*; *Gates Of Eden* was already completed.

In New York he often hung out with Bob Neuwirth. Neuwirth was another psychedelicized mind, cynical but still amusing. He and Dylan saw together that the world was dominated by vast interests, manipulated by amoral people who killed and cheated with cheerful abandon in the quest of power. They saw that from the top to the bottom the same system operated. Dylan's songs sprang now from that point of view – an eye floating over the city of the unclean, the crazed rich, the miserable and the mean.

Occasionally they ventured into the new epicenter of hip, which had definitely drifted away from Folk Music circles into Pop Music and Pop Art circles. Andy Warhol was now operating from the Factory on E. 47th Street. Doctor Roberts was giving his famous injections in midtown, not far from Max's Kansas City, which was the "in" night zone for hip madcaps and pranksters. These injections of Doctor Roberts were popular with almost everyone in the elite and consisted of a startling array of vitamins, tranquilizers, methedrine and other kinds of speed. Equally startling was the Doctor's clientele, which included politicians, along with agency chieftains, rock 'n' rollers and debutantes galore.

Beatlemania was in full frenzy in the USA. The "British Invasion" was seriously underway; British rock groups were pouring across the Atlantic just as fast as their managers could arrange US tour dates. In the American hinterland too there were stirrings, with early groups like the Blues Project, a seminal New York outfit organized by Danny Kalb the guitarist, who were appearing in small clubs. The impetus towards rock was already strong.

During these months, Bob was moving around on a wide social horizon. At one end he connected (via Ginsberg) to the world of the "underground", the heritage of the beat generation that Allen and Jack Kerouac had been mentors to. Ginsberg's oft-stated desire to fuck Bob Dylan also exposed Bob to a new form of homosexuality, openly stated, out of the closet, that was beginning to appear.

Uptown, he was in great demand for parties and was occasionally seen in the circles where record company executives dwelt, moving through the gilt-edged seam of Manhattan's liberal elite.

Yet, he was also seen down in the Village at folk music hoots.

He still liked to take his guitar and go down and play for his peers, the other folksingers. Here he could expose the new songs – songs that were often vehicles for poking fun at the people he met – the women who came and went.

He was in perfect step with a changing tide of consciousness that was at that moment filtering through the baby boom generation as it matured. Bob Dylan found himself, perhaps unconsciously perhaps not, setting down the ground rules emotionally, and to a degree intellectually, for the following cohorts. Even such heavily charged acronyms as SDS and LSD were replacing protest and Mod, so copies of *Another Side Of Bob Dylan* were prominently displayed in the rooms, studies and dorms of hip American youth in the fall of '64.

On another front, things weren't going quite so well. He continued to struggle with *Tarantula*, a book that he owed Macmillan's and which kept changing shape. In the beginning, according to Dylan, *Tarantula* was a response to book offers and a sizeable cash advance from publishers panting to get something out of the new bonanza in Folk popularization.

"We took the biggest one, and then we owed them a book. You follow me?"

In April '63 he told Studs Terkel that Tarantula was "about my first week in New York. Not about the big city really, the Big City's got nothing to do with it. It's about somebody who really has come to the end of one road, knows there's another one there but doesn't exactly know where it is."

This idea didn't really work either, and Dylan decided against having it published. He took it back from the publisher and re-wrote it. It got looser and looser too, becoming what Dylan called "collages", a variant on William Burroughs' "cut-up" technique.

On October 31 he gave a concert at the New York Philharmonic Hall. It was a great success and a stereo PA tape was made, which has escaped and become a bootleg record of excellent sound quality called *All Hallows Eve 1964*. A double album, it preserves forever a great moment in Dylan's rise to the heights. There are eighteen songs recorded, three sung with Joan Baez in the second half and they range from *The Times They Are A Changing*, with which he opened the concert, to *Mr. Tambourine Man*, *It's Alright Ma* and *Gates Of Eden*. In the second half he reverted to the songs of *The Times They Are A-Changin'* and the three he regularly accompanied Baez with: *Mama You Been On My Mind*, *With God On Our Side* and *It Ain't Me Babe*.

At one point he stopped after the introduction to *I Don't*

*Believe You* and asked someone to give him the first line since he'd forgotten it – someone did and he got on with it. Later, when someone called out a request Dylan replied: "I'll do anything, hope I never have to make a living."

Since he'd given up his own apartment in Manhattan, Bob stayed with friends in New York City, or in hotels. The rest of the time he stayed at Grossman's place in Woodstock. In November he went to California and played a number of dates: Berkeley again, then San Jose and Los Angeles. Joan Baez appeared as his unannounced guest. While he was there Sing Out! magazine came out with a long, impassioned "Open Letter to Bob Dylan". Written by Editor Irwin Silber, it begged Bob to reconsider his ways and go back to playing "protest" type Folk music. However, Silber noted the growth of Bob's "entourage" and worried about the "self destruction" which he feared might emerge. "A lot has happened to you in these past two years, Bob – a lot more than most of us thought possible." But Silber, rooted in his own love of Folk music, unamplified, stemming from the old roots of the culture, was deaf to what was coming. Bob knew that he, Dylan, was already bigger than Folk could ever be in popular terms. He was nurturing ideas for the next step that he knew would alienate the folk music business even more.

Back in New York he met Sarah Lowndes, a friend of Sally Grossman, Albert's young wife (who is pictured with Bob on the cover of *Bringing It All Back Home*). Sarah was an ex-model, living alone with her daughter in the Chelsea Hotel. She was very interested in eastern religions, had a mystical side that appealed to Bob. At this time he was using the I-Ching and investigating Buddhism. They hit it off very well, Sarah apparently made no effort to use her friendship with Dylan to impress anyone else. This of course impressed Bob a great deal.

Not long afterwards, Bob took a room in the Chelsea Hotel himself to be close to her.

However, he still roamed the scene, usually with Neuwirth. In December, according to Neuwirth, they called up Edie Sedgwick, the young debutante daughter-of-the-year, who was already cutting up the Manhattan scene as a "youthquaker". They all met in a Village bar. Edie came in a limo, of course, and had a splendid time. Dylan continued to see Sedgwick on and off over the next year or so and Edie gradually entered a relationship with Neuwirth.

A few months later Edie Sedgwick became Andy Warhol's favorite movie 'star' and began appearing in Andy's movies.

For a brief while her flame dazzled the scene, before the drugs wore her down and the fashion skipped on.

In early '65, Dylan began recording the next album, his fifth. To be titled *Bringing It All Back Home*, it marked a radical departure. On Side One he cut a quartet of out and out rockers, including *Subterranean Homesick Blues* and *Maggie's Farm*, and throughout there are drums and a restrained little combo of studio musicians at work. On Side Two he put the songs written in the previous summer and fall, and he used Bruce Langhorne, a noted guitarist of the time, to lay a gracious, lovely guitar sound around his own playing.

Dylan's anger comes through clearly; the music was drenched with fearsome images, crazed humor and a slightly bitter acceptance of the way the world works.

In February he appeared on the Les Crane TV show with Bruce Langhorne to back him. Les Crane asked Dylan what he spent his money on and Dylan looked at him a moment and said, "Boots, bananas, fruit and pears."

Later that month Joan Baez swung into the east on her current tour. They linked up again and began a formal joint concert tour. The harmony between them, however, was not as perfect as it had been. The managers feuded from the start, as neither Grossman nor Emanuel Greenhill liked the poster originally painted for the tour by Ric von Schmidt, both seeing the other's client as somehow projected more favorably. This continued.

Bob had grown increasingly paranoid, frequently given to fits of arrogance, as the pressure of being the King of Folk bore down on him. With Baez, he began to have tantrums. In response, she became motherly which only made him worse.

Part of it was that he knew, in his roots as it were, that the direction Joan was heading in, via the Institute of Non-Violence she'd founded in Carmel, California, was inherently wrong-headed. The system was vast and powerful and resting on trillions of dollars. The men and women who owned and ran it were not going to be brought down by any mass movements. This was not France in 1789.

Most importantly, Bob's songs were about Bob now, and the way the world was on the inner horizons. Through everything now he felt the pull of the Tao, the mystical sense of balance that runs through the word, the dharma void and every buddhist's imagination.

In these concerts with Baez, Bob was doing a set combining elements from the past with a central chunk that usually ran *Gates Of Eden, If You Gotta Go Go Now, It's Alright Ma (I'm Only*

79

*Bleeding)*, *Mr. Tambourine Man*. Then he'd go back to *Don't Think Twice It's Alright*, *It Ain't Me Babe*, and other older songs before ending with *It's All Over Now Baby Blue*. Together of course they only sang the older songs.

The new album came out in March and caused quite a considerable stir. On the cover, Dylan reposed in sophisticated style, the background was patrician down to Sally Grossman, his manager's wife, sitting beneath an ornate mantelpiece bearing items of esoterica. The austere look of *Another Side* and *The Times They Are A-Changin'* was gone.

The cat that Dylan cuddled, by the way, was his own called Lord. Later one of its offspring was to die in a fire at the Chelsea Hotel that also almost killed Edie Sedgwick.

On the back, Dylan published a longish poem concerning the ways of the world and his attempts to deal with it. It's hard to say whether he thought he was succeeding, but it does seem clear that he was enjoying it.

The songs themselves, with all that whirling imagery, really stirred up the mass audience and the critics. The use of a rock outfit was another self-perceived slap in the face for the Folk devotees, but the record sold very well. Bruce Langhorne's guitar work received due acclaim; Bob's densely packed lyrics reverbrated through Rock music circles. This was it. This was the direction to capture the fever of the times.

The gigs with Baez continued, although as some witnesses from then have commented: "There were constant blow-ups, it was very touch and go." Emotionally, there was turmoil as well. Legend has it that Dylan proposed marriage to Baez and that she said 'no thanks.' Possibly Joan had seen too much already of the infamous Dylan ego of this period. In an interview with Anthony Scaduto, she said that though they'd joked about marriage, it'd never been a real proposal. They had been very close, but they were pulling apart now.

He finished the month of April with some engagements in the west, appearing at places like the Civic Auditorium in Los Angeles. He did not appear with Baez at these shows.

In early May he went back to England again for another tour. This time he was accompanied not only by Baez and the managers, but also by a film crew and Director Pennebaker who made the documentary film *Don't Look Back*, during the ensuing tour.

Things were not going well between Dylan and Baez. In fact, as she later lamented, he'd decided along the way that he didn't want her there. "He wouldn't let me sing," she said. What had been conceived of as a continuation of their joint tour now became a solo Dylan tour. Baez hung around, feeling silly and oppressed by this, for a week or so and then walked away from it and went to visit her parents in France. She'd found that Bobby had suddenly become impossible to deal with, cutting everyone else out of it. As recorded in the film *Don't Look Back*, Dylan seems to ignore everyone around him to a certain degree, except for journalists that he skewers and some hapless loon who is verbally stripped down for throwing a glass.

The loon bleats "You're a Big Noise – you know?" Bob replies: "I know it man, I *know* I'm a Big Noise!" The rest of the time Bob pounds the typewriter or takes the stage.

Apart from the soundtrack to *Don't Look Back* which was bootlegged, a tape of part of his Royal Albert Hall show that May has reached bootleg form – *Long Time Gone* EPs – and contains a similar set to that from the early American stages of the tour.

In June he appeared on a special two-part BBC TV broadcast. The setting was slightly too formal to be really comfortable and Bob appeared quite reticent between songs, except to introduce *It's Alright Ma* with "ho ho ho, it's a funny song."

He also did *Hollis Brown*, then *Tambourine Man*, *Gates Of Eden* and nine others, ending with *It's All Over Now Baby Blue*.

In England, Bob Dylan found he had stirred an audience just as fanatical and aroused as that in the USA. Earlier in the year *Subterranean Homesick Blues* had been a top ten hit in England. English folkies abounded however who knew all Dylan's stuff backwards but despised his move to electric rock.

But the harder sound of rock that he heard in England in '65 confirmed him in his urge to get a bigger sound around him, to use amplified instruments and the new rock technology that was spearheading the new sound. Apparently while in England, he even went into CBS' Bond Street recording studio and tried some things out with some members of John Mayall's Blues Band. If true, then this provides an interesting counterpoint to the developments that awaited on the other side of the Atlantic.

Many years later, Dylan said of *Don't Look Back*:

> It was somebody else's movie. It was a deal worked out
> with a film company but I didn't really play any part in it.
> When I saw it in a movie house I was shocked at what
> had been done. I didn't find out until later that the
> camera had been on me all the time.

Dylan also claimed that it was one-sided, that it was "a

propaganda movie" and that though the scenes depicted in *Don't Look Back* did occur, those were "early days". Presumably he's much nicer nowadays.

However, the Pennebaker film did convey the strangeness of touring, the harsh alienating sort of life that one and two night stands can produce. Moreover, this was a critical moment in Dylan's personal life, increasingly divorced from his public one. When Baez split for France, Sarah Lowndes was in England and taking care of Bob who had gotten sick under the pressure of it all.

The tour finally finished; the film was in the can, complete with a few creative touches from Bob such as his holding up the cards that read things like 'Basement', and he turned his attention to the next step. As can be seen in *Don't Look Back*, Dylan was writing furiously most of the time. He had a whole new bunch of songs and he needed a rock band, something that would take him further than Bruce Langhorne and the studio musicians on his last outing.

He and Sarah were living up in Woodstock together. He called Mike Bloomfield, among others, and Bloomfield came to play a pivotal role in the events of the next couple of months. The period that saw Dylan rise above his generation and the rock scene and even take a single to the top of the pop charts, while simultaneously spurring a huge controversy among his older fans. Bloomfield said years later:

> I went to Woodstock, and I didn't even have a guitar case. I just had my Telecaster and Bob picked me up at the bus station and took me to his house where he lived, which wasn't so much, and Sara was there I think, and she made very strange food, tuna fish salad with peanuts in it, toasted, and he taught me these songs *Like A Rolling Stone* and all the songs from that album.

Soon they met up again in New York City. Bloomfield was slotted to record with Dylan and so was Al Kooper who played keyboards and some guitar for the Blues Project. Bloomfield also got to see how the In-group around Bob operated. He observed to Ratso Slocum during a phone interview that, "Bob, Albert Grossman and Neuwirth had this game that they would play and it was the beginning of the character armor, I think, it was intense put downs of almost every human being that existed but for the very few people who were in their aura that they didn't do this to... They had a whole way of talking."

In the studio they had Bobby Gregg on drums, Russ Savakus on bass; Bloomfield strummed his electric blueswailing guitar, albeit restrained, and they cut *Like A Rolling Stone* and the rest of the next album. Entitled *Highway 61 Revisited*, this was Bob's homage to his own roots of rock and but for *Desolation Row* on side two it was all patently rock.

Discussing *Like A Rolling Stone*, Dylan told journalist Jules Siegel:

> I wrote it as soon as I got back from England. It was ten pages long. It wasn't called anything, just a rhythm thing on paper – all about my steady hatred directed at some point that was honest. In the end it wasn't hatred. Revenge, that's a better word. It was telling someone they didn't know what it's all about, and they were lucky. I had never thought of it as a song, until one day I was at the piano, and on the paper it was singing "How Does It Feel?" in a slow motion pace, in the utmost of slow motion. It was like swimming in lava. Hanging by your arms from a birch tree. Skipping, kicking the tree, hitting a nail with your foot. Seeing someone in the pain they were bound to meet up with. I wrote it. I didn't fail. It was straight.

While they were recording *Highway 61 Revisited*, a Dylan song sung by West Coast folk-rockers, the Byrds, was hitting Number One nationally. *Mr. Tambourine Man* was the first real "Folk-Rock" hit and spawned an entire sub-genre of follow-up groups. Dylan however, with Bloomfield and Kooper, was cutting much harder material altogether.

Throughout '65, Columbia had been releasing 45s by Bob Dylan but with scant success in the pop charts. In Britain and Europe *Subterranean Homesick Blues* had been very successful but in the US, Columbia had continued to play to Bob's folk audience, releasing *Gates Of Eden* backed with *She Belongs To Me*, *The Times They Are A-Changin'*, backed by *Honey Just Allow Me One More Chance*. These sold creditably but did not crack the top twenty by a long shot. *Maggie's Farm* released in May had done better still, but it would be *Like A Rolling Stone* that finally did the trick. Originally it was backed by *Gates Of Eden*, then a second pressing was released with *Rolling Stone* on both sides.

The name *Bob Dylan* was all over the radio; *Mr. Tambourine Man* had suddenly magnified his sales appeal enormously and *Like A Rolling Stone* took off very quickly.

This success produced changes in Albert Grossman's touring strategy. It was an axiom of Grossman's that hard work by a performing act was the name of the game in becoming a success, and touring was never more profitable and useful than when an act was riding chart success. Albert's plans for the autumn and winter became ever more grandiose.

It also produced much thought concerning the make-up of a touring band to back Bob and the new songs. In the studio Bloomfield and Kooper had been terrific but they were both strong stylists with reputations of their own, they had strong egos.

There was also a group called the "Hawks" that John Hammond recommended. The Hawks were Canadians, who'd coalesced originally behind Ronnie Hawkins, a Rock 'n' Roller from Arkansas who'd toured Canada extensively enough to wind up with a Canadian group backing him. They'd split with Hawkins and had spent plenty of time on the road doing their own stuff, they were well seasoned. Dylan met them, got on very well in particular with Robbie Robertson the guitarist, and started playing with them practise sessions.

They had been "discovered" by John Hammond Jr., who was pursuing a career as a white bluesman. On his second album *So Many Roads*, recorded for Vanguard, the Hawks provided good solid backing.

At the end of July, Bob was due to appear at the Newport Folk Festival once more. Also on the bill was the Paul Butterfield Blues Band, a Chicago outfit playing authentic- sounding electric blues. Bloomfield was on the point of joining Butterfield, having had no offer from Dylan. The Butterfield Band, however, were only performing on the sunday afternoon, a quiet part of the festival given over to new acts.

At the Festival, jammed with Dylan fans torn by the controversy over the new rock Dylan, Bob and the Butterfield Band practised together back stage and had a great time. Bloomfield had his Telecaster and knew the songs and managed to drive the group in the right sort of direction. Bob made a fateful decision, buoyed by these sessions. He invited the Butterfields to back him on stage during part of his performance. The Butterfield Band was dying for a chance to play to a big crowd, and not just the little sunday afternoon one, and they jumped at the opportunity.

Bob kept this a secret, at least from the crowd, and surprised everyone when he turned up on stage with several members of the Butterfield Band and Bloomfield, and they plugged in and ripped into a pretty untogether version of *Maggie's Farm* with Bloomfield's guitar howling away.

Naturally, Newport wasn't used to this, nor was the

microphone turned up loud enough and Bob was drowned out in the backwash of the Butterfields.

The confusion was increased when people near the stage started calling for the mike to be turned up so they could hear the words, and then people at the back who didn't want to hear rock music at the Folk festival picked up on it and began yelling and booing.

It seemed that Dylan had misjudged the audience; when the band finished a barely recognizable version of *Like A Rolling Stone* there was hardly any applause. No one was hearing much beyond boogie. After *It Takes A Lot To laugh, It Takes A Train To Cry*, there was more yelling and booing. Shouts of "Get your folk guitar" cut through and Dylan, who admitted later to being "stunned", left the stage for a while. The Butterfields melted away and the crowd was left either stunned itself or in turmoil. Then Bob came back on and performed *It's All Over Now Baby Blue* and *Mr. Tambourine Man*.

A stereo SPA tape of this performance escaped into bootleg form and appeared as *Passed Over And Rolling Thunder*. At the end of the acoustic numbers, the audience applauded very enthusiastically. Off stage though, a feeding frenzy was underway among the critics. Fallout from the festival continued for the rest of the year. The Folk establishment reacted as if stabbed in the back. They'd reared a viper in their midst. Dylan professed unconcern:

It doesn't bother me", he told Vogue. "These people who claim to be old fans picked up on me a year and a half ago. My old fans, the ones in the Village five years ago, they'll understand. I can't keep painting the same picture. I could please them it's very simple. What would it be worth – it would be putting them on. I'm not experimenting – been playing for fourteen years. I know what I'm doing, I played rock 'n' roll when I was thirteen.

Dylan told Robert Shelton of the New York Times:

If they can't understand my songs, they're missing something. If they can't understand green clocks, wet chairs, purple lamps or hostile statues, they're missing something too." He also said: "What I write is much more concise now than before. It's not deceiving."

But the war raged on. On August 27, Dylan pulled fourteen thousand spectators to Forest Hills tennis stadium in Queens, New York. Dylan and Grossman had resolved to do it properly this time. They went early in the day and took a lengthy sound check. An historic photo session took place at the same time.

For this show, Dylan selected a group leaning towards the Hawks. Robbie Robertson on guitar, Levon Helm on drums, with Al Kooper on keyboards and Harvey Brooks on bass.

Come performance time, Dylan set out to ease the audience into it. He did seven acoustic numbers from *She Belongs To Me* through to *Ramona* to *Desolation Row* and *Tambourine Man*, in all forty-five minutes of non-electric material. The crowd applauded thunderously.

At the interim he told the musicians, "Anything can happen with that crowd.... don't let it bother ya. Just keep playin' the best you know how."

There were boos and a small but vocal minority that kept yelling for older songs but Dylan kept it driving along, audible this time, and by the end of the set he had most of the audience firmly with him.

In the electric half of the set, along with *Just Like Tom Thumb's Blues*, *From A Buick Six*, *Maggie's Farm* and *Rolling Stone*, he did an electric version of *It Ain't Me Babe*.

*Like A Rolling Stone* was Number One, on its way to becoming a gold record. Bob Dylan had scaled the pinnacle he'd set out to climb as a fourteen year-old, along the way he'd changed the rules for writing rock songs and by accident, spawned Folk Rock as well.

In October Dylan gave another concert at Carnegie Hall. Again there was an acoustic first half and an electric second half. The true fans were out, there was no booing. Unfortunately, no tape of this show nor that at Forest Hills has made it into bootleg form or been released officially. They must have existed though; maybe they still do.

He selected the Hawks to accompany him on the great tour that Albert had planned. However Levon Helm did not join them. Nor did Bloomfield and Kooper, both now pursuing their own projects.

When moving around now on the scene to pop parties and art showings and Warhol movie presentations, Bob was accompanied by David Cohen, who later began singing professionally under the name David Blue. Cohen supplemented Neuwirth's company for these expeditions. Cohen told Scaduto:

> Dylan was very hostile, a mean cat, very cruel to people.
> Dylan was super-defensive, his privacy had been
> invaded. It was just too heavy for him, being the center
> of attention, having people all around asking things and

demanding answers. The crowds scared him now and he hated it.

On November 22, Bob married Sarah. It was a small ceremony, performed by a judge in Nassau County in suburban Long Island – Grossman and a lawyer and one or two friends. It was not announced, not even to Dylan's close group of friends in New York. He was determined to create some area of privacy for himself.

# CHAPTER SEVEN

## Like A Rolling Stone

In the latter half of 1965 Bob Dylan became an international phenomenon. His records were being played everywhere, his picture loomed from a thousand magazines. He was quoted endlessly by the young and the hip and the *avant-garde*. Stepping out of the in-grown little world of folk music to rack up chart hits that changed the patterns of rock lyricism forever, he'd reached that zenith he'd desired since the days in Hibbing.

He had album sales of half million units with both *Bringing It All Back Home* and *Highway 61 Revisited* on the album charts at Nos. 6 and 3 respectively. *Like A Rolling Stone* reached No. 2 in the singles charts and sold a million copies worldwide to become his first Gold Record. He was spoken of in the same breath as the Beatles and the Rolling Stones, the new giants of rock. Mind you, there were unusual aspects; Dylan never set up a Fan Club, never hired a Public Relations person, he refused to have anything to do with the hype mill, only going so far as to hire a young lady to sort through the mail.

Magazine writers converged on him now like wine experts on a rare vintage. They wanted to know precisely what he meant by it all. So did their readers – there was a palpable thirst for explanations, for Dylan's thoughts. However for the most part they were to remain mystified. But they did get snap shots of the physical Dylan of the time. Ralph Gleason, preparing an interview article that appeared in Ramparts magazine, described him thus:

> The contrast between Dylan the person and Dylan the prophet of the Doomsday Poems is startling. Thin, almost emaciated, his lips clutching a cigarette, he talks quickly and nervously in a distinctive edgy softness, using the language of the hip street folk. His hands are cold and he seems shy and quick, like a young deer...

Now Dylan found that the pressure he'd experienced over

the past couple of years from folk fans and fame was magnified ten-fold. Now he simply could not appear in public. When he had to go out, someone would go and flag a taxi, and then after a check for lurking fans or photos on the sidewalk, Bob would dash for the safety of the cab.

Mail arrived in torrents, much of it demanding to know what his songs meant anyway. Other artists were recording his songs wholesale, or else imitating his approach as closely as possible. Square media kept announcing to the world that he was now doing what it called "Folk Rock". Bob responded, "I can't use that word, that Folk Rock, that's not me." One singer called Mouse actually had a hit with a song called *A Public Execution*, that copied Dylan's delivery, lyric style and sound so closely that many people bought it, believing that it *was* Dylan, just doing something mysterious by putting out records under another name.

There was pressure from Columbia for more product; he was hot and they especially wanted another hit 45. The charts of '65 were jumping with radically new and aggressive sounds, and the record company wanted Dylan to compete. The Rolling Stones, for example, were chart-topping with *Get Off My Cloud* – their breakthrough hit *Satisfaction* was still on every juke box in the land. The Beatles meanwhile had the *Rubber Soul* LP at No. 1 and the movie *Help* doing fantastic box office throughout the summer. Over in England, a new group called The Who was surging to the fore with *My Generation*.

There was pressure from the publishers, Macmillans, demanding something – a book, any kind of book – to put out, and of course there was pressure from his peers, who wanted to see if he could keep it up, keep writing stuff that would simultaneously knock every competitor out of his socks *and* hit the Top Ten.

Furthermore, since he'd become part of the cutting edge of the cultural changes that were polarizing America, he was also the target for a lot of hostile questions from the press. With the hostile and the just plain dumb, Bob now evolved a playful, but devastating method of counterattack. The setting was usually a press conference, of which he gave several in the course of the year.

The pattern was set during the English tour. When quizzed about "the Message" in his songs in April, Bob said the message was "keep a good head and carry a light bulb." At the San Francisco press conference in December he was asked if he was "primarily a singer or a poet." He replied: "Oh I think of myself more as a song and dance man."

"A what?" said the bemused interrogator.

"A Song and Dance Man" quoth Bob. "Why?", asked the reporter. "Oh, I don't think we have time to really go into that", concluded Dylan.

At a conference in LA, things got more hostile. Someone actually asked, "Bob, you sing mostly love songs. Is love important to you when you write the songs?"

Dylan: "No."

Trying another tack the reporter pressed on, determined to extract the secret. "Then is it more important to you when you sing the songs?"

Dylan: "No."

In Austin, Texas, he was asked: "Well, what do you consider yourself? How would you classify yourself?" He replied: "Well I like to think of myself in terms of a trapeze artist."

Again in L.A. there was this famous exchange. "Bob is it true that you dedicated your first song to Brigitte Bardot?"

Dylan: "Yes, it's true."

"Why? Why did you do that?"

Dylan: "Why?"

"Are you a fan of Brigitte Bardot?"

Dylan: "Yes, of course."

"Why?"

Dylan: "Why? (laughter) Do I have to answer that? I mean you have to think for yourself a little bit."

And so it went, but during this period Dylan gave many interviews and press conferences and generally made himself available to his public in a way that he was never to repeat. Wherever possible, he sought to try and answer worthwhile questions crisply and as openly as possible. But he grew less and less charitable to the idiots.

Yet he had an urge to try and explain himself and what had been going on within him during this momentous year. He'd felt the force of the reaction that his switch to rock had brought on. He'd seen the sterility of his continuing as a folksinger, in an era of expanding rock possibilities. He spoke at length about his feelings of guilt over appearing as a folksinger, when in his heart he was dying to get a band and rock out.

In the Ramparts interview he did with Ralph Gleason he said:

> *Rolling Stone* is the best song I wrote. I wrote *Rolling Stone* after England. I boiled it down, but it's all there. I had to quit after England. I had to stop and I knew I had to sing it with a band. I always sing when I write, even prose,

and I heard it like that.

Again to Jules Siegel in another interview he explained:

> After I finished the English tour, I quit because it was too
> easy, there was nothing happening for me. Every concert
> was the same; first half, second half, two encores and
> then run out, then having to take of myself all night.
>
> I didn't understand. I'd get standing ovations and it
> didn't mean anything. The first time I felt no shame. But
> then I was just following myself after that. It was down
> to a pattern.

To break the pattern, Bob turned to rock and the poet's route.
"You have to vomit up everything you know. I did that. I
vomited it all up and then went out and saw it all over again",
he told Ginsberg and Gleason. "I'm willing to try anything once
– Doing things for kicks, that's why I do things, without
hangups."

To friends who hadn't, he said:

> You gotta read the I-Ching. I don't wanna talk about it,
> except to say it's the only thing that's fantastically true.
> You read it and you gotta know it's true. It's something
> to believe in.

And to everyone he stoutly maintained, "Of course, I don't
believe in anything."

The cries of "sellout" continued to echo from the folk cellar
but Dylan ignored them. Allen Ginsberg however commented:

> Dylan has sold out, to God. That is to say, his command
> was to spread his beauty as wide as possible. It was an
> artistic challenge to see if great art can be done on a juke-
> box. And he proved it can.

Whatever he believed in, Bob didn't seem to care much about
the tried and true formulae when it came to building on his
chart success. In September '65 he released a follow-up to *Like
A Rolling Stone*. this was *Positively 4th Street*, a long, snarling
tirade, a vintage Dylan put-down. Incredibly, this record
actually made it to No. 7 on the pop charts and sold a quarter
of a million copies. Radio DJs and programmers were taken
aback, *Positively 4th Street* was an out-and-out nasty, almost
vicious song, certainly the meanest thing that had ever made
the Top Ten, normally a realm of dreams and wistfulness. Bob
was taking a crack back at the army of folk music critics that
had made such a commotion about his shift out of "protest"
with *Another Side* and then his move to rock. They'd booed him,
jumped on his mistakes like the appearance at Newport with
the Butterfield Band, and now he gave it back to them. With

*Positively 4th Street* snarling out of radios and jukeboxes that fall, the Dylan haters had to take their lumps, a galling experience no doubt.

However, close friends and would-be competitors like Phil Ochs, were dismayed. Ochs thought that Dylan "blew it" at this point. That he shut the door to the sort of gigantic commercial success of Elvis Presley or the Beatles. But Dylan doesn't seem to have cared too much about it, or to have thought that his appeal would last that long. In Chicago, in November, he said:

> I'm going to say when I stop, it just doesn't matter to me. I've never followed any trend, I just haven't the time to follow a trend. It's useless to even try.

Still Israel Young was attacking him in the columns of the East Village Other, an underground magazine, and hundreds of folk fans were writing to Sing Out! to mourn "the death of Bob Dylan, who died at Carnegie Hall on October 1, 1965" and so on.

But Bob had no time left for the folkies, "Folk Music is a bunch of fat people", he growled at one interview. Besides, he was now deep into Albert Grossman's grand tour scheme, an exacting schedule that took him across the country and through Canada twice in six months.

The press conferences continued too. Bob turned up for these ordeals clad in the now familiar uniform of huge prescription sunglasses, suit and boots. He dismissed the unhip questions but did say some things very clearly:

> The protest thing is old, and how valid is it anyway? Is it going to stop anything; is anybody going to listen? People think this helps, but songs aren't gonna save the world.

Slightly less clearly he also said:

> Folk Music destroyed itself. Nobody destroyed it. Folk Music is still there, it's always going to be there, if you want to dig it. It's not that it's going in or out. It's all the soft mellow shit, man, that's just being replaced by something that people know is there now. Hey, you must've heard rock and roll long before the Beatles? You must've discarded rock and roll around 1960. I did that in 1957. I couldn't make it as a rock 'n' roll singer then. There were too many groups....

In October he did an interview with Allen Stone in Detroit and said:

> Now it's different, now I want to play the songs because

I actually dig them myself. Whereas I was doing a lot of
stuff before which I didn't really dig because I had
written them so fast and under such very weird, strange
circumstances.

By December, he was back on the West Coast on the last loop
of the second tour and did a set of nine more concerts there
which grossed ninety thousand dollars something of a record
for those times. By now he was getting pretty pale; he'd always
been skinny, but after his schedule went into that high touring
gear, one nighters, two nighters, and then back to the jet, on
to the next city, Bob became somewhat unhealthy looking.
Moreover, to help him get up and on stage, and to help him
remember all the words to all the songs he was using a
considerable amount of amphetamine. When the speed ran
down he had to take other things to ward off the depression
and stay human. Of course this was 1965, when anyone could
be jailed for years just for smoking marijuana, so Bob was
decidedly reticent concerning the drug topic. Besides which the
levels of perception on the opposite sides of the culture chasm,
between straight press reporters who hated rock 'n' roll and
everything that went with it and drug users themselves, were
so widely seperate that no worthwhile communication was
possible.

In L.A., the press conference was full of hostiles and cretins.
They attempted to grill him on the subject of drugs. He told
them he didn't need drugs, that he had a "nervous disorder".
Things got weird...

> Q: This is a personal question and I hope you'll forgive it,
> but you sound and you look very tired. Are you ill, or is
> this your normal state?
> Dylan: Well I take it as an insult! I don't like to hear that,
> that kind of thing.
> Q: I don't mean to offend you but we can hardly hear
> you and you look weary.
> Dylan: Well I'm from New York City and you're all from
> California and you have this health thing....

The press continued to bore in, seeking the truth about dope:

> Q: Some of your critics say that you have no real purpose
> in mind when you write and sing except to shock people.
> Dylan: Now, you know that's not true. You've heard the
> songs haven't you?
> Q: Yes.
> Dylan: Well, you know that's not true then.
> Q: I think *Puff The Magic Dragon* and *The Family Man* were

considered by some to be endorsements of marijuana smoking.

Dylan: Well, I didn't write *Puff The Magic Dragon*, that's a horrible, that's a, I didn't write that whatever that is. I didn't write that. And *Mr. Tambourine Man*. There's no marijuana in that song, at least, I've never heard of it before.

Another subject that had straight media up in arms at the time was sexual freedom. In San Francisco therefore Dylan was asked:

Well do you participate in the new theme? Sexual freedom and so forth?

Dylan: I don't participate in anything (laughter). Nothing! I bet you couldn't name one thing that I participate in. Go ahead, I dare you! (laughter).

The press backed off unable to raise any blood, still mystified by it all. The pressure however was still on him; he had to come up with new songs for another album and Columbia were demanding a new single. At the end of the California leg of the tour he holed up in a big house in the Hollywood hills called the "Castle" and worked furiously on new songs. He went into the studio with the Hawks in L.A. and they cut at least six and perhaps many more than that, new tracks, including: *Can You Please Crawl Out Your Window*, which was released as a single in mid-December. The rest of what is known of this session turned up in bootleg form and included a lovely song then titled: *Seems Like A Freeze Out (Visions Of Johanna)*, which differed from later versions in that it had the extra words "in the nightingale's code" in the last verse. There was also an eerie, rather lovely backing track which has come down, entitled: *Number One* on the bootleg records and which may be the backing for the missing Dylan song, the legendary *The Church With No Upstairs*. Also from this session came a couple of rockers, including another one hundred octane, vitriol number called *She's Your Lover Now*, which was briefly considered for a single and then discarded.

*Can You Please Crawl Out Your Window* continued the evolution of Dylan's sound that had begun with *Bringing It All Back Home*, continued through the Bloomfield/Kooper sessions and *Like A Rolling Stone* and was to peak with the next album, *Blonde On Blonde*. The lyrics too were vintage Dylan, of the cryptic and surreal variety, but it seems they were just too complex for 1965, a veritable dense pack of Dylan mysteries, invective and put downs.

94

Radio programmers gave it little airplay and it rose only to No. 58 in the charts before subsiding in January '66.

"I never did care much for singles", Dylan told Jan Wenner of Rolling Stone Magazine in 1969, when discussing this period in his career. He felt the pressure of having to come up with a single and found it most unwelcome. Before this, the songs had just poured out of him when he wanted them, when it was right for them to come. Now they *had* to appear, on schedule, and pass judgement on the radio.

However, he shrugged off the disappointment and while back in New York after Christmas, he recorded again. *Sooner Or Later (One Of Us Must Know)* was rushed out, with *Queen Jane Approximately* on the B side, to plug the gap, but it too failed to move on the charts.

Still Dylan was recording whatever the time allowed it now, and writing new songs in between recording sessions and engagements. In early January, he had *Leopard Skin Pill-Box Hat*, soon afterwards there was *4th Time Around* and *Absolutely Sweet Marie*. He was recording in Nashville, Tennessee, with a group of professional studio men grouped around Charlie McCoy and Kenny Buttrey.

When in New York for rare periods of relaxation, he rejoined his (still secret) wife Sarah. They were moving out of the Chelsea Hotel and shopping for a townhouse. Sarah was going to have a baby. They settled on a house in Manhattan's East Thirties, and for the first time Dylan actually owned his home.

Home life however was but one facet of things for Bob, he still found time to make the Manhattan scene. On expeditions into the vortex of hip he was accompanied by the same tight little group of friends and fellow singers, like Neuwirth, Dave Cohen, Phil Ochs and Eric Andersen.

One night Phil Ochs fell from grace. Dylan played the new single, *Can You Please Crawl Out Your Window* for Ochs and Cohen, telling them "this is the one I've been trying to do for years, this is the record that's really got it."

Ochs was unimpressed however, he knew it wasn't a hit single and he said so. Dylan reacted badly, unable to take any criticism from Ochs, who they both knew imagined that he could make it big, that he might compete with Dylan. "It's a great song. You only know protest?" said Dylan with some anger.

Ochs, it was true, had stuck to the protest sub-genre, within the confines of the folk movement and had had some success there too. His *There But For Fortune* had been a minor hit for Joan Baez for example.

Later that same night they were ensconced in Dylan's limo, heading uptown, when Dylan suddenly ordered Ochs out of the car. "Get out Ochs, you're not a folksinger, you're just a journalist." Ochs was horrified, numbly he got out of the car. Ochs was cut from Dylan's circle from then on.

When out and about on the scene now Bob was talking about movies. He wanted to do another film and there were plenty of people eager to get him into a film project. However, he wanted to have control over any film he did. Doubtless the enormous success the Beatles had had with *Help* had reinforced Bob's urge to make a movie soon.

One tantalising, potential avenue for a hit film was presented by the dynamic debutante, Edie Sedgwick. The undisputed "star" of Andy Warhol's Factory films, Edie was bored with Andy and his cheap little movies, she'd made a dozen of them and seemed to possess a star quality that many people noticed. She wanted to move on to something bigger and better and was casting about for some way to do this.

Among those who were interested was Albert Grossman. He turned up at the Factory one day, supposedly to watch Nico sing. Nico had met Dylan in Europe and with her ex-model's figure and ultra-fine bone structure, she was now regarded by some as the coming thing in New York's avant-garde. However, Grossman did not pursue Nico, who soon wound up singing with the Velvet Underground instead. Albert was more interested in Edie and asked Warhol's minions for a showing of some of Edie's Warhol movies. Shortly afterwards, Grossman signed Sedgwick to a contract, at Dylan's urging it was said, and Edie said goodbye to the Factory for good.

In "Edie – An American Biography" Jonathan Taplin, a scenemaker of the time, was quoted as saying:

> Dylan liked Edie because she was one of the few people who could stand up against his weird little numbers; she was much stronger than the sycophants who were hanging around him at the time. He was always in an adversary relationship with women. He tested people, perhaps to find out about himself....

Nico was later to say that *Leopard Skin Pill-Box Hat* was written for and about Edie Sedgwick, and certainly it is known that Dylan, Neuwirth and Sedgwick hung out together at parties and social events at this time. Dylan's cat had sired some kittens and Bob gave Edie one; she named him "Smoke." He was to die about a year later in Edie's Chelsea Hotel fire.

*Previous page:* Nashville Skyline

*Left:* Dylan in 1965

*Right:* Dylan in 1963

*Below:* With Joan Baez
and Paul Stookey at Lincoln
Memorial – August 1963

*Above:* At a party in London where he was presented with two awards – Best Folk Music Record for 1964 and Best Newcomer to Records

*Above right:* With Joan Baez in London's Embankment Gardens, April 1965

*Above:* With Johnny Cash on US TV, 1969

*Above:* Sitting in the audience at a Leon Russell concert, Newhaven, Ct. 1972

*Below:* At Blackbush with Eric Clapton

In Sheridan Square, Greenwich Village, NY – January 1965

*Above:* Dylan and his wife Sara (left) with George Harrison and his wife

*Below:* With Dinah Shore

*Above:* 1971 – Dylan and friends

*Below:* **The Band's Last Waltz** – with (left) Van Morrison and (right) Robbie Robertson

In Pat Garrett

*Above:* Dylan and Mike Bloomfield at a recording session

However, one thing that Bob seems to have avoided telling Edie about was his marriage. It is said that Andy Warhol was the one to break the news to Edie, having heard the story from an agent. It is also said that she was rather shaken by the news.

Despite all the talk and the plans, Dylan was never to make a film with Edie, or any kind of scripted movie of the conventional kind. He turned instead to Howard Alk and they made plans to do something more on the lines of *Don't Look Back*. Edie moved on to make a film with Bob Neuwirth instead, another cheap, spontaneous film. Later she was to become the star in *Ciao Manhattan*, a bizarre epic that captured something of the strange intensity of her world in Manhattan during these years.

Meanwhile, the pressure grew on Bob to fulfill his publishing contract and with it there came an awareness that the literary establishment was virtually drooling in anticipation of getting its hooks into *Tarantula*. Macmillan's didn't really care, they just wanted something to publish. John Lennon's pair of slender, humorous volumes had sold marvellously well. Dylan would surely do even better, they knew his audience had a high literacy percentage.

In early '66, the New York Times turned its attentions to Dylan and the claims made for his poetry. They took the trouble to line up several poets with university postings to either denounce him or praise him. What they would do with *Tarantula* could easily be imagined.

By now, Dylan had been dragging this book around for several years. He admitted he had problems with it. In Detroit he'd said:

> I can't use the ideas they're so deformed and, and just not really right ideas. Stuff which has been expressed you know, a million times, you know, in the past....

*Tarantula* wasn't about to go away however, and he was forced to try and come to grips once more with the thing. In his 1969 interview with Wenner, Dylan described what happened:

"I got it back to proof read it. I got it back and I said: 'My gosh did I write this. I'm not gonna have this out. I'm not gonna put this out.'" So it was re-written again but the new book didn't impress him either, "I just looked at the first paragraph – and knew I just couldn't let that stand. So I took the whole thing with me on tour. I was going to re-write it all. Carried a typewriter around the world...."

One interesting sidelight on the *Tarantula* question is the existence of photos purportedly taken for the jacket of the book. These featured Dylan and a few objects Dylanesque, propped outside a rural shed somewhere. From the shed's interior peers Edie Sedgwick, wrapped in a shawl.

The tour dates kept coming too. In February, Dylan and the Hawks were doing concerts up and down the East Coast. The set at this time was organized in much the same way as that of late '65 except that *Desolation Row* and *Visions Of Johanna* (the other title *Seems Like A Freeze Out* had been dropped) were the long songs in the acoustic half of the set, replacing *Gates Of Eden* and *It's Alright Ma*. He still finished that half with *Mr. Tambourine Man* and *It's All Over Now Baby Blue*.

In the second half, with the Hawks, he did *Tell Me Mama, I Don't Believe You, Baby Let Me Follow You Down, Just Like Tom Thumb's Blues, One Too Many Mornings* and *Leopard Skin Pill-Box Hat*. For encores they did *Like A Rolling Stone* and *Can You Please Crawl Out Your Window*.

By now, his secret marriage was a secret no more. Nora Ephron broke the news in a New York paper and many of Dylan's close friends were completely taken by surprise – he had told no one about it.

In March, Playboy Magazine published a long interview with Bob conducted by Nat Hentoff. Apparently this interview was the subject of quite a struggle between Dylan and the Magazine and was only published after Dylan and Hentoff did considerable rewriting of it. As it ran though, it encapsulated a lot of Dylan's feelings at the time. It is clear that he was utterly weary of the whole idea of revolution through song, that he saw no way to change the world except in the Taoist manner, by each person changing themselves within. He had nothing more to say on the subject of why he'd switched to singing rock, reeling out a long strand of surreal nonsense in response to the question, "What made you decide to go the rock 'n' roll route?"

Again, when told that former fans were charging that "you vulgarized your natural gifts" Dylan replied:

What can I say? I'd like to *see* one of these so-called fans. I'd like to have him blindfolded and brought to me. It's like going out to the desert and screaming, and then having little kids throw their sandbox at you. I'm only twenty four. These people that said this, were they Americans?

In this interview he also said quite clearly:

I'm not a New Yorker. I'm North Dakota – Minnesota – Midwestern. I'm that color. I speak that way. I'm from some place called Iron Range. My brains and feelings have come from there. I wouldn't amputate on a drowning man; nobody from out there would.

Hentoff asked Bob if he would like to become President of the USA. Dylan replied: "No. When I was a boy, Harry Truman was President. Who'd want to be Harry Truman?" However he did concede that *if* he ever did become President there would be some changes made:

> Just for laughs, first thing I'd do is probably move the White House. Instead of being in Texas, it's be on the East side in New York. McGeorge Bundy would definitely have to change his name and General McNamara would be forced to wear a coonskin cap and shades. I would immediately re-write the *Star Spangled Banner* and little school children instead of memorizing *America the Beautiful* would have to memorize *Desolation Row*. And I would immediately call for a showdown with Mao Tse Tung; I would fight him *personally* – and I'd get somebody to film it.

Also in March he got down to Nashville for further sessions with McCoy, Buttrey, Joe South and the rest of the studio band. Together they were getting the sound that he described years later thus:

> The closest I ever got to the sound I hear in my mind was on individual bands in the *Blonde On Blonde* album. It's that thin, that wild mercury sound. It's metallic and bright gold, with whatever that conjures up. That's my particular sound....

At last, the *Blonde On Blonde* collection was coming together. In addition to the songs recorded earlier he now had *Obviously Five Believers*, *I Want You*, *Memphis Blues Again*, *Just Like A Woman*, *Pledging My Time* and *Sad-Eyed Lady Of The Lowlands*. Concerning *Sad-Eyed Lady* he told Wenner:

> It started out as just a little thing, *Sad-Eyed Lady Of The Lowlands*, but I got carried away, somewhere along the line. I just sat down at a table and started writing. At the session itself, I couldn't stop. After a period of time I forgot what it was all about and I started trying to get back to the beginning....

Once he'd finished in Nashville, Grossman pointed Bob and the Band back onto the road for yet another marathon schedule of dates. First to the West Coast once more, then to Hawaii for a gig in Honolulu, and then on to Australia in the third week of April. There, beginning in Brisbane on the 15th they did seven gigs in nine days, fielded incredibly hostile press conferences, traversed the continent and finished up in Perth, Western Australia on April 23.

A mono PA tape of the acoustic half of one show in Melbourne escaped onto the bootleg market and appeared as *Bob Dylan In Melbourne Australia*. It includes *4th Time Around*, *Visions Of Johanna*, *It's All Over Now Baby Blue* and *Desolation Row*. Dylan sounds as though *4th Time Around* might better be described as *4000 & 4th Time Around* and he takes plenty of time to tune up a borrowed guitar, but he sings well if just a little bit laid back, throughout. By this time, after a year or more of pretty continuous touring, recording and travelling, the strain was taking a toll.

While in Australia there was some unwelcome news from home. First they heard that Paul Clayton, the folksinger, had jumped out of a window on LSD, and then that Richard Farina, whose book *Been Down So Long It Looks Like Up To Me* had become a classic of hippy bohemia, was dead in a motorcycle crash. Farina had married Joan Baez's sister Mimi, he and Dylan had been friends for years and Bob was definitely shaken by the news.

However, the tour stretched ahead of them. From Perth they flew on to Stockholm, Sweden, to begin the European leg. While in Europe they were to rendezvous with Howard Alk and Richard Pennebaker to shoot a new film, to be called *Eat The Document*, which was contracted now for ABC TV and a series that was planned for the following year.

The logistics involved in all this, moving Dylan and the Band around from continent to continent on time, keeping them sane and alive and out of the clutches of local police forces, plus organizing the filmmakers and their end of things, must have been mind-boggling. Albert Grossman had become the great Mastermind of the Schedule, moving all with precision. The gigs stretched on into the future, endless. Dylan however was starting to run out of steam.

Another aspect to the tour now was that in Europe and Britain audiences came expecting the Folk Music Dylan. The booing and ugly audience reactions that Bob had endured in the previous year in the US were now recreated in Paris and London. After the Parisian concerts a French newspaper ran a banner headline screaming "Bob Dylan Go Home!" and proclaiming he was a "dead idol" for French fans. In Britain there were some fraught scenes as well, especially at the Royal Albert Hall, where Dylan's performance yielded up one of the most sought after of all bootleg records. Here Dylan was confronted once more with a small but vocal bunch of folkies who yelled their displeasure during the electric half of the set. Bob got progressively more surly about it and then after *Ballad Of A thin Man* towards the end, a voice rang out from the crowd, crying "Judas!" Dylan snarled, "I don't believe you, you're a liar". The Band began the intro to *Like A Rolling Stone*, Dylan leaning back from the mike – shouted "a fucking liar" and then he and the Band roared into an astonishing version of *Rolling Stone* with all the passion left in their bodies, one of rock's ultimate moments from the sixties.

The electric half of this concert turned up on a tape of excellent quality, even with stereo, and spawned bootlegs like *Zimmerman – Looking Back, In 1966 There Was*. From other gigs in Britain and Ireland more tapes and boots have come down, plus one superb 45 side of *Just Like Tom Thumb's Blues* that was released by Columbia as the B side of *I Want You*. From the Dublin Adelphi concert came a tape of the acoustic set; from Edinburgh came an audience tape of the whole concert. The set was similar to that of the last tour in the US with the addition now of *Just Like A Woman* in the acoustic half and *Ballad Of A Thin Man* in the electric half.

While in Britain they shot a mass of footage for *Eat The Document*. Grossman had parlayed the idea into the ABC TV show for a one hundred thousand dollar advance. Basically, Dylan and the Band played their dates and Alk and Pennebaker shot film. A lot of other short scenes were spliced in as well. Dylan was later to say of this experience: "My film concept was all formed in those early days when I was looking at that footage."

In the summer of 1968, Dylan discussed this film project at some length with John Cohen and Happy Traum. The results were published in Sing Out! that autumn. Sing Out! by this time had managed to forgive Dylan for his earlier defection from Folk. Of the making of the film Bob said:

> Mr. Pennebaker's eye put together *Don't Look Back*,
> whereas someone else's eye put together this film....
> What we were trying to do was to make a logical story
> out of this newsreel-type footage... to make a story
> which consisted of stars and starlets who were taking the
> roles of other people, just like a normal movie would
> do... that's not what anyone had in mind, but is what
> myself and Mr. Alk had in mind. And we were very
> limited because the film was not shot by us but by the

"eye".

However, *Eat The Document* was never to be screened. "The program folded" in Dylan's words, and "by the time we handed it in, they had already begun a state-wide search to confiscate the film, because it was the property of ABC. So we were a little pressured here and there..."

In *Eat The Document*, there was a swift parade of very short cuts, ten seconds, thirty seconds, constantly shifting. Fragments of Dylan with the Band doing things from the tour set were intercut with a blizzard of other stuff. Many people appear and disappear, among them John Lennon who says the word "money" from a car window.

While in London on this trip, Dylan saw John Lennon several times, visited Lennon's luxurious suburban home and together they discussed their situation and the horrible problems it brought, the pressure, the endless touring, the need to take speed and tranquilizers, heroin, anything to cool off that pressure after a gig.

The tour was finally over; the film was finished and Bob and the Band headed back to America. There, *Blonde On Blonde* had been released as a double album – quite a commercial risk for the time – but heavy initial sales propelled it into the album charts anyway. From the album Columbia put out an edited version of *Rainy Day Women No.12 & 35* as a single, backed with *Pledging My Time*. It quickly entered the charts; it was unforgettable – Bob Dylan's party record – but the party might just be in the asylum. This was the summer of '66; the US was up to its hips in the blood and mire of Vietnam; taking drugs, in particular smoking marijuana, and listening to Dylan records, especially *Blonde On Blonde*, became a form of national antidote to Vietnam for an entire generation, as they waited to see if they'd be called up for the army.

Their world was getting out of hand, moving beyond insane. The ghettoes of American cities were exploding. Five hundred thousand young Americans were in the 'Nam battling the Viet Cong and the North Vietnamese Army in a war that few understood and even fewer really desired. Having *Rainy Day Women Nos. 12 & 35* in the top ten on the radio, seemed perfectly appropriate.

It appeared that Dylan was back on top of the pressure once again. Not only was he No. 2 in the singles charts but *Blonde On Blonde* had made it to No. 9 in the album charts and looked set to repeat the sales success of *Highway 61*. He was taking a month's vacation, staying up in Woodstock with Sarah. Things looked bright; he was free of the old Columbia contract now as well and Al Grossman was shopping around for a new company. A deal was in the air with MGM, involving a million dollar advance. He was soon to be a father too – Sarah was expecting.

However, there were still problems. *Tarantula* was one. Dylan was working on the book once more. Then trouble developed in the MGM deal. It seemed MGM was worried about the rumors of drug addiction, and about Dylan's bad press, he was at the least a non-patriotic figure and it was a time of tension between patriots and those who were against the war. Then a time-bomb turned up in the Columbia contract in the form of a percentile that had been missing from Dylan's royalty payments for years on all his albums subsequent to the first, *Bob Dylan*. Columbia owed him a considerable sum of money, and gathered together into one huge payment in 1966 – if Dylan signed with someone else – it would largely go to Uncle Sam in income taxes.

Then before either the contract or *Tarantula* could be dealt with, disaster struck. On July 29, Dylan, out riding on his motorcycle, with Sarah and/or friends driving behind in a car, lost control of the bike, skidded and was flung out of the seat and into the road. Somehow they scraped him off the highway and got him into the car and took him to Middleton Hospital about twenty miles away. He was found to have crushed neck vertebrae, he was in concussion and his face and neck were lacerated.

The rock 'n' roll world was stunned by the news. Just as so many stars had been taken before in accidents, it seemed now that Dylan too was going to die. The rumors began at once, ranging from the simple if morbid "Dylan is dead, they just haven't released the word yet..." to the paranoiac "The CIA wanted him dead, they all wanted to get rid of him, he was dangerous..."

The truth, however, was that Dylan still lived. He spent a week in the hospital and a month in bed at home; he had come close to death but had survived.

# CHAPTER EIGHT

## Woodstock & Big Pink

Sitting around his new chateau in Woodstock for several months in a neck brace and dressings, Dylan had time to reflect on things.

It seems he was primarily grateful to be still alive. He was also a father – Sarah had borne him a son, whom they christened Jesse Byron. He brooded somewhat on the mechanics of his career. What had once been a fairly pleasant sort of fame, set in a career of regular small tours and times for recording had swollen into a hysterical monster. The endless touring had made him question Al Grossman's plan, even his motives. Naturally Dylan had become very successful going by Al Grossman's book, but if Bob went crazy or died by accident as a result, what was the point? Dylan also felt abused by the contract hassling that was going on. There was tons of money, certainly – Bob had done his part of the deal. All his records were in print, all were selling. In a seven-year stretch he'd been intensively productive, pumping out seven albums, eighty odd recorded songs and probably another one hundred and fifty that Dylan didn't record for one reason or another. In addition, he'd made hundreds of appearances; had completed four and a half tours of the USA; performed at folk festivals; appeared with Joan Baez and completed three tours of Britain, two of Europe, and even one of Australia.

Dylan had exhausted himself for "them" and now all that was happening was a lot of squabbling with lawyers and accountants and publishers.

As he saw it, the cost of all that work, especially in the last year, had been the need to take a lot of speed, a lot of junk, a lot of tranquilizers and booze, just to keep aloof from the horror of it all. If you could stay stoned then you could handle it, but to perform for yet another hallfull of eager, but critical fans, you had to get *up*, and that of course had mental and physical consequences. On top of which lay the paranoia, of everything from local cops to weirdos that wormed their way into dressing rooms and hotels.

Like most punk stars have done, especially those who are happily married at the time, it seems he concluded that it was one helluva life he'd been leading. Condemned to a zillion hotel rooms that looked the same, daily airplanes and airports, more jet lag than you could shake a boarding pass at, and finally the fans and the hostiles. Each group took an effort to deal with, each was relentless in its quest for answers.

Obviously this was very likely to kill you or make you prematurely old. He decided he'd had enough of it, at least for a while. He wanted to be with Sarah; he was in love. He decided to shut the doors of his private life and exclude the world.

The silence set in. Not a word escaped about Bob Dylan over the ensuing months. The rumors rolled by, the business deals continued and the negotiations with MGM grew difficult, but the records continued to sell and *Blonde On Blonde* was an international hit now. The sound that Dylan had helped refine, from the electric blues and Langhorne-aided "folk-rock" of *Bringing It All Back Home* was acclaimed as timeless, majestic, beautiful. *Highway 61 Revisited* and *Blonde On Blonde* were both records that would stand forever, beyond fashion and temporary fame.

The weeks became months and the scene rolled on. Dylan became even more of an icon, a mythic figure in retreat in the woods. In New York, things were shifting fast to decadence – the era of the Chelsea Hotel and the Velvet Underground had begun. Perhaps Nico's ethereal groaning on Lou Reed's song *All Tomorrow's Parties* on the first Velvet Underground LP captured it best. The debutantes of *Like A Rolling Stone* had long ago done their deal with the "mystery tramp." Doctor Roberts and his injections had even made it onto a Beatles album. The Chelsea Hotel, a long-time haunt of literary types and actors who couldn't afford an uptown hotel, was not filling up with folk poets and rock 'n' rollers. In October '66, Edie Sedgwick moved into the Chelsea when her parents cut her allowance off.

Also in October *Don't Look Back* was screened at last and Dylan fans got a chance to see Bob going through the motions on the '65 tour. It was already historical, and tenderly viewed as such by the rock press, a new phenomenon on its own. The scene was exploding outwards now; new talents were emerging everywhere. In the summer of '66, at Windsor Festival in England, the first "supergroup" was formed. Cream, as it was called, boasted Eric Clapton, the foremost white electric blues guitarist of his time, plus Ginger Baker and Jack Bruce, both veterans of the British blues and rock scene. Cream took that Clapton guitar around the world. A few months later, Jimi Hendrix appeared in Britain under the wing of manager Chas Chandler, who had once been an 'Animal' with Eric Burdon and Alan Price. Hendrix took electric guitar off on a soaring trek into space, sound and time.

Out in San Francisco, an unearthly number of strange looking young Californians had gathered to celebrate the use of LSD in the Acid Tests, during which the Grateful Dead played. Other groups were stirring, like the Jefferson Airplane in San Francisco and the Doors and Love down in Los Angeles.

And equally noteworthy was another kind of evolution in Rock. In August, a rock group put together for a TV show, the Monkees, debuted with their first hit record *Last Train To Clarksville*. The visual impact of the Beatles' films *A Hard Day's Night* and *Help* had produced a echo in the corporate world of television. The alienating 'system' that permeated the culture had responded swiftly to the fresh scent of money. The same system that Dylan had impaled so often in song now had rock fully understood.

Rumors about Dylan continued to come and go. Dylan was alive it was generally conceded, but he was a zombie who would never record again. Or Dylan was in a coma – it was being kept secret from the record companies until Al Grossman got the million-dollar deal he wanted. There were endless permutations, of which many verged on the utterly mad.

Yet Christmas came and went; the MGM contract vanished into thin air, and still there was no word from Bob Dylan. Even the cynics began to wonder if the rumors were true in some way? If Dylan had been left a zombie then, of course, he wouldn't be recording. If he wasn't a zombie, then how does one account for the uncharacteristic silence?

The enigma continued to torment the concerned right through the winter; the mystery deepened with the passing months. It wasn't possible for someone like Greta Garbo to disappear from the public eye, not in the world of Rock! Yet that seemed to be what was happening.

Finally on May 8, '67, a reporter for the New York Daily News, Michael Iachetta, tracked Dylan down to his house in Woodstock.

> After four hours of driving up narrow mountain trails,
> running from watchdogs, getting stuck in the mud and

106

winding up hopelessly lost, you get a straight answer and you are there, impressed by the brooding wealth of the mahogany-stained estate you see in front of you.

On that first occasion, Iachetta was sent away, but he came back the next day and knocked on the door again and was rewarded with the sight of Bob Dylan, behind a screen. Dylan took a moment to remember Iachetta from an interview done long before and then invited the reporter in. He refused to let a photographer in though: "It's one thing facing a writer, but I have this hang-up about cameras now."

So it was confirmed. Dylan was alive, busted up a little and definitely in seclusion. Further interviews were zealously discouraged: "Dylan is alive. Dylan is not seeing anybody", said Grossman's office to all inquiries.

But Dylan was getting active again; he was certainly seeing Bob Neuwirth, who was commuting regularly up to Woodstock to look at the footage of *Eat The Document*. As the summer wore on, Dylan started driving over regularly to West Saugerties from Woodstock, where the Band had taken a house called 'Big Pink'. The Band had dropped the name the Hawks, and had also called Levon Helm back from Arkansas, where he'd gone while they were touring the world with Dylan. In the basement of Big Pink, they set up instruments, got a couple of reel-to-reel recorders and practised together. With Dylan, they proceeded to record at least twenty-four songs – songs like *This Wheel's On Fire*, *I Shall Be Released*, *Nothing Was Delivered* and *You Ain't Goin' Nowhere*.

This was music about mystery, as Greil Marcus was to write in the liner notes that eventually accompanied it on official recording:

It is a plain-talk mystery; it has nothing to do with mumbo-jumbo, charms or spells. The 'acceptance of death' that Dylan found in 'traditional music' – the ancient ballads of mountain music – is simply a singer's insistence on mystery as inseperable from any honest understanding of what life is all about; it is the quiet terror of a man seeking salvation who stares into a void that stares back...

Eighteen of the twenty-four songs somehow escaped Dylan and the Band's control. Once bootlegged under the name *Great White Wonder* and mixed in with tracks taken from earlier bootlegs right back to the Minnesota Hotel Tape of '61, the material hoisted the bootleggers out of the collector's groove they'd been in and made bootlegging a big business on its own.

The activity, though, was all kept from public view. Dylan remained aloof from the world and his public throughout 1967. Sarah was pregnant once again; she was to have a little girl this time, they named her Anna. Dylan was a contented father, and his only immediate task came from Grossman which was to render a new album to supplement a new recording contract. Somewhere along the line he had abandoned *Tarantula*. The book was shelved, when he read this it pained him; he decided that song writing was his artform, he would leave books to other writers.

The need for a product to convince wary record companies that Dylan could still do it – still make million-selling records – and wasn't some rubbed out zombie who was past it, made Grossman push Dylan. In an interview later Dylan said: "I was being *pushed* again" (Dylan's emphasis) to come up with songs. This was part of the old life, the madness of '65/'66, that he had resolved to avoid, this pressure was something he hated. Possibly that feeling of being pressured again contributed to a feeling he developed that summer, a belief that he told Jan Wenner about a couple of years later:

> I still didn't realize the importance of the accident till at least a year after that. I realized it was a *real* accident. I mean, I thought I was gonna get up and go back to doing what I was doing before but I couldn't do it anymore.

Columbia had put out a couple of singles, things from *Blonde On Blonde. Leopard Skin Pill-Box Hat* only made it to No. 81 early in the year and in the summer a re-issue of *I Want You* and *Just Like A Woman* was released to little interest. There was however some interest apparently from Otis Redding, by then just beginning to break through the racial barrier in pop music and achieve a wide success with a white audience. Otis requested a copy of *Just Like A Woman* and apparently intended to record it before his untimely death in December '67.

A year had gone by and Dylan's disappearance was a widely accepted fact. The scene had moved on – others had taken up the challenge. The Beatles had brought out *Sergeant Pepper's Lonely Hearts Club Band* that spring, the end product of a marathon recording sesion with all manner of "psychedelic" effects and lyrics. The Beatles had broken the mould for pop music just as thoroughly as *Blonde On Blonde* had the previous year. It is said that the first time this new Beatles record was played for him, Bob listened to a few cuts and then ordered it turned off. He later explained that he couldn't hope to master the intricacies of such full usage of the recording studio, for he didn't understand the technical tricks of such brilliant sound effects, as he was just Dylan, someone who sang songs. If it couldn't be done with a little rock group and his voice, then he wasn't about to do it.

In addition, he did not have unlimited access to any recording studios. In the sixties there were few independent studios, very little mobile recording equipment, the technology for making records was controlled by the major companies and they used that control for leverage.

Meanwhile the scene that had given Dylan such vivid images and hallucinatory brush strokes for his last three records, had exploded beyond the confines of Manhattan, San Francisco's Haight Ashbury and London's Rockocracy. LSD was now illegal everywhere but there was more of it than ever and hippies by the thousands were appearing in new psychedelicized ghettoes in the major cities of the Western world. From Amsterdam to Los Angeles, from Edinburgh to Boston, long-haired youths, "acid rock", young women in mini-skirts and floral patterns; these were the new clichés of media outrage, the so-called "summer of love."

And while they demonstrated against war, against nuclear weaponry and repressive Police and drug laws, these young-sters defiantly risked mind and body with drug experimen-tation. They wanted for themselves the same Poet's search described long before by Rimbaud, the same search for the Self in the mysterious ocean of being that Dylan had made and reported on through four albums.

Not surprisingly, Bob's records, especially the last three, continued to sell very well throughout 1967 and they were played constantly, over and over, as listeners tried to pierce the ambiguities, the double entendres and the hidden identities on Dylan songs.

Columbia put out *Bob Dylan's Greatest Hits* that summer and it immediately hit the charts and reached No. 10. The contract hassling was over. Dylan would sign once more with Columbia, despite Grossman's wishes.

The "summer of love" was also a summer of heat in the black ghettoes of the USA. Racial tensions were high as young black men, enraged by their condition, thrust fists skywards and called for "Black Power." A frightened white establishment reacted predictably, with gunfire and jail sentences. The fall-out was widespread. On June 19, 1967, for example, Rubin Carter and a friend John Artis, both black, were jailed in New Jersey for supposedly killing three whites in a hold up the year before.

The evidence was shaky but Rubin "Hurricane" Carter was a boxer with a reputation for supporting "Black Power." An all-white jury sent him away.

By the autumn of '67, posters of Bob Dylan – big blown-up photos of Bob in dark shades or psychedelicized "artworks" – were selling so briskly around the youth culture that Dylan's image became as pervasive in hip homes as Mao Tse Tung's was in China.

Some poster manufacturers made enough money out of Dylan's posters to commence small publishing businesses. The underground press used Dylan as a continual visual selling point. A hundred million pictures of Bob Dylan were being sold and marketed and printed and, of course, Bob himself received absolutely nothing from any of this. Meanwhile the bootleggers were working overtime, as not only were his songs being bootlegged, but a manuscript of *Tarantula* escaped into the Dylanophile market and was swiftly samizdated by the hundreds.

Naturally his prolonged absence from public view contributed to the power of the myth, but Dylan continued to live in seclusion with wife and kids. At this time, we must assume that to Bob, the most important thing in the world was Sarah and the children and the salvation she offered from the madness he had come from. Her gentility, his happiness, a mutual appreciation of things Zen and mysterious, of the quiet in the heart, and the whisper of divinity underlying all life, all of this served to heal Dylan as he was later to recount it. He came to see his survival as a miracle. Years later in an interview he said:

> Well I was straining pretty hard and couldn't have gone on living that way much longer. The fact that I made it through what I did is pretty miraculous. But you know, sometimes you get too close to something and you got to get away from it to be able to see it. And something like that happened to me at that time... Those were in my wild unnatural moments. I'm glad those feelings passed.

Again in an interview in 1974 with Mary Travers he said:

> The turning point was back in Woodstock. A little after the accident. Sitting around one night under a full moon, looked out into the bleak woods and I said "something's gotta change."

It seems clear now, from the strength of Dylan's reaction against what he'd produced in the previous couple of years – a reaction he manifested in interviews for years afterwards – that the idea of peeling himself down layer-by-layer, while flaying everyone around him for lyrics and lyrical characters, had soured on him. He'd decided against competing anymore in the International Rock 'n' Roll stakes.

He turned against rock now with an acuteness that was to take everyone by surprise. As disconcerting to some fans as his previous turns against "protest", and then folk music itself, had been. Many years later he was to say in partial explanation, "my being Gemini explains a lot. It forces me to extremes, I'm never really balanced in the middle. I go from one side to the other without staying in the either side place for very long."

Now the thought of performing songs like those he engaged with the Band seemed wrong. That would simply mean re-entry into the rock 'n' roll madhouse with inevitable comparisons between what he was doing and what the Beatles and the Rolling Stones were doing. Then the pressure would grow for him to tour again, go back on the road and the endless hotel rooms.

In late September early October, he went down to Nashville again and recorded with Kenny Buttrey, Charlie McCoy and Pete Drake on steel guitar. There were a couple of sessions over two days and they cut twelve new songs. He returned in November and December to apply finishing touches. He chose an obscure photo for the cover, showing a bashful-looking, smiling, bearded Bob Dylan, in a winter wood scene with a couple of escapees from some Woodstock Indian Ashram and some white fellow with a leather hat. The cover was grey; the picture was black and white, which bore on the back a little mystery parable. It was titled *John Wesley Harding* and it caught the expectant world of fans and critics by surprise.

For a start, it was definitely not a rock album. This was rock with a small 'R', even country-rock. Compared to the output of the strongly-rated groups of the time, the Doors, Jefferson Airplane, the Beatles and the Rolling Stones, *John Wesley Harding* was decidedly different. A relaxed little combo, Dylan used a lot of piercing harmonica, along with lyrics which indicated that Dylan had reached some kind of accommodation with the vision he had earlier expressed in awe and fury. Songs like *I Dreamed I Saw St. Augustine* and *The Wicked Messenger* were philosophical farewells to Dylan's previous incarnation. He clearly intended to mark a turning of corners, maybe even a temporary retirement from the scene. *All Along The Watchtower* gave a promise of other things to come, and new directions Dylan might turn towards.

Released at the beginning of '68, it soared swiftly to the No.

2 spot on the US album charts. Dylan seems to have given up the desire to put out hit singles, for no single was released at this time. Nor did Bob break the wall of silence that he'd imposed on the media. He made no tour plans, no future plans at all that were publicized.

Naturally, there was some fallout with Albert Grossman over this. It is said that Grossman cared little for the record, or the direction that Dylan was taking. Grossman didn't hold with cutting oneself of from the sort of success Dylan had had. Grossman also wanted Bob to tour again, after eighteen months lay-off there was such an enormous pent-up demand for Dylan concerts that any manager would have been champing at the bit.

It seems a struggle built up between Grossman and the commercial world out there and Sara and the domestic world in the home; Bob came down on Sara's side.

However, Dylan did come out of retirement for one performance that year. On January 20, 1968, he appeared at the New York Woody Guthrie Memorial Concert. This was to be the first of two such concerts, another one was held in Hollywood. Bob came on with the Band, who were disguised on the billing as the Crackers (for contractual reasons) and performed three numbers with them, *Grand Coulee Dam*, *Mrs. Roosevelt* and *Ain't Got No Home*, all sung in a rock 'n' roll style. Since this burst of rocking came in the midst of a folk concert by such stars as Judy Collins, Pete Seeger, Arlo Guthrie, Odetta, Tom Paxton and of course Ramblin' Jack Elliott, it was clear that Dylan was making no concessions yet to the spirit of the Folk Movement.

Family life, home cooking and so forth had certainly changed Bob's appearance. He looked a little heavier than he'd been before the accident, as his hair was neatly parted down the middle and he sported a beard on the underside of his chin. The contrast with the former Dylan persona – he of the tumbled mane of curls, inscrutable dark glasses, suits and boots – was striking.

The three tracks he played with the "Crackers" were included on the *Tribute To Woody Guthrie Part One*, which was released by Columbia. *Part Two*, without Dylan & the Crackers, was recorded in L.A. by Warners and released by them. In addition to the cuts with the Crackers, Bob was induced by Odetta, publicly pleading with him on stage, to sing a verse in a group version of *This Train*. However this rarity exists only a collector's tape and has yet to appear on vinyl.

After the show, Bob went back to Woodstock once more.

Meanwhile, the songs that he'd recorded with the Band during the previous summer and withheld from release were being cut by other artists, especially in Britain. Julie Driscoll was to have a big hit with a version of *This Wheel's On Fire* and Manfred Mann took *Mighty Quinn* to No. 4 in the US singles charts and No. 1 in the UK.

The interest in Dylan's music and his intentions showed no sign of slacking, although his lack of public interest in such issues as the Vietnam War was hurting him in the underground press and in those circles that were concerned with politics and wars.

In May his father, Abraham Zimmerman, died. Dylan went back to Hibbing for the funeral and stayed a few days with his family. Not long afterwards, Sara gave birth to another child, a boy they named Seth Abraham Isaac Dylan.

In June and July, Bob met with John Cohen and Happy Traum and recorded a lengthy interview in which they discussed things like *Eat The Document* and *John Wesley Harding*. They talked about whether the new songs could be called ballads. Dylan:

> Well I do, but not in the traditional sense. I haven't fulfilled the balladeer's job. A balladeer can sit down and sing three ballads for an hour and a half. See, on the album, you have to think about it after you hear it, that's what takes up the time, but with a ballad, you don't necessarily have to think about it after you hear it, it can all unfold to you. These melodies on the *John Wesley Harding* album lack this traditional sense of time. As with the third verse of *The Wicked Messenger*, which opens it up, and then the time schedule takes a jump and soon the song becomes wider. One realized that when one hears it, that one might have to adapt to it. But we are not really hearing anything that isn't there; anything we can imagine is really there. The same is true of the song *All Along The Watchtower*, which opens up in a slightly different way, in a strange way, for here we have the cycle of events working a rather reverse order.

Later, in the same interview, Bob talked about "work", and his intention to keep doing some:

> ...and to make the work interesting enough in order to keep doing it. That's what has kept it up so far. I really can't do it if it's not interesting. My intention would be not to think about it, to block it up somehow, I've discovered this from the past anyway. There was one thing I tried to do which wasn't a good idea for me. I

tried to write another *Mr Tambourine Man*. It's the only
song I tried to write 'another one'. But after enough
going at it, it just began bothering me, so I dropped it. I
don't do that anymore.

They discussed poets and Dylan owned to liking Blake, Dante
and Rilke. Throughout the interview, Bob came over as relaxed,
seemingly without cares. When asked what he might do in the
near future he said:

Well... I've been toying with some ridiculous ideas, just
so strange and foreign to me, as a month ago. Now some
of the ideas – I'll tell you about them after we shut off this
tape recorder.

Had Dylan already begun to explore the idea of making a
new, simpler kind of music? To cut an album of love songs with
simple themes, or even to record other peoples' songs?

The Cohen/Traum interview appeared in Sing Out! in October
'68. That summer also saw the release of the Band's first album
on their own, entitled: *Music From Big Pink*. It boasted a Bob
Dylan painting on the front cover, a picture of the house 'Big
Pink' inside and some wonderfully exciting music on the vinyl.
It received very good reviews and sold very well, reaching No.
30 in the US album charts. It established the Band as a force on
their own. Their second album, *The Band*, reached No. 9.

In November, George Harrison and his family visited the
Dylans up in Woodstock. The Beatles had started Apple,
pooling their interests and resources in a formal, corporate way.
They'd put out the 'Double White' album *The Beatles*. It is said
that George and Dylan got on very well and, when visiting
England in '69, Bob and Sara stayed with the Harrisons. Dylan
played George some new songs, and on Harrison's successful
solo album *All Things Must Pass*, Dylan is credited on *I'd Have
You Anytime*.

It appears possible that Dylan also took some singing lessons
around this time. He told Eric Andersen that he'd learned to
sing properly for the first time in his life. However, he was also
to say that the change in his singing voice which occurred at
this time could also be laid to the fact that he'd given up
cigarettes.

At the end of '68, Dylan formed a new music publishing
company called Big Sky Music, a company wholly owned by
Bob himself. Thereafter, he proceeded to Nashville and began
recording the first few songs for his next album, which at this
point had no title or clear identity. He informed Jann Wenner
later that year ('69) that, initially, when he went to Nashville,

he had just four songs and for a while things began to click. The sound of modern Country Music was appealing too, a new vehicle for Dylan. With Johnny Cash he did some practise dubs and from them came the idea of recording *Girl From The North Country* together. Reputedly a joint Cash/Dylan album was discussed by Columbia for official release, but Dylan avoided that after due consideration. However in February '69, he and Cash held a session and recorded at least twelve songs that later escaped to the bootleg market under the title *The Dylan Cash Session*. This comes in stereo with excellent quality throughout and thus may well have been recorded in a Columbia studio.

In January, Dylan appeared with Cash in the Johnny Cash Documentary for TV. They sang *One Too Many Mornings* together. As a novelty, their duet was great, but it was clear that their voices didn't match particularly well and that Bob's harmony singing was pretty straightforward stuff.

Nonetheless, after *Nashville Skyline* was released in April, Dylan went back to appear on Cash's show, The Johnny Cash TV Special on ABC. According to some who saw this show, Dylan's first live TV appearance in years, he looked "Absolutely terrified", but he sang his three songs *I Threw It All Away*, *Living The Blues* and a duet with Cash on *Girl From The North Country*.

Terrified or not, Dylan had created some useful publicity for his album, appealing to a whole new market – the Country market – as well as his old fans. On the rock scene the album was causing quite a stir. The critics savaged it – many of them finding it hard to believe that Dylan could put out a record of little more than "product" songs that lacked the earlier Dylan imprimature of message and mystery. There were no mysteries on *Nashville Skyline*, just pleasant good-time music and country homilies.

Nevertheless, it sold very well and reached No. 3 on the US album charts very quickly. A single *I Threw It All Away* was released to little action and then someone had the wit to put out *Lay Lady Lay* as a 45 and Bob woke up to find he had a top ten hit once again. *Lay Lady Lay* reached No. 7 on the singles charts that summer and went on to become a standard on juke-boxes all over the Western World.

If the bad reviews had troubled him, such good sales figures must have gone a long way to reassuring him that he hadn't made a fatal mistake.

That spring, it became clear that Bob was not going to re-sign with Albert Grossman. Gossip concerning who his future manager might be swirled in the pop music circle but no announcement came. Subsequently, Dylan dropped Grossman and managed his own business affairs, he has not had a manager since.

At about the same time, he began to tell friends that the simple country life in Woodstock was beginning to pall. Even worse, the place was filling up with rockers and film people while house prices rocketed. Al Grossman was opening a restaurant and negotiating with Warners for his own record label, eventually to be called Bearsville. There were rumors that a horribly big messy Rock Festival was going to be held in Woodstock that summer and that as many as half a million fans would show up.

Bob, Sara and the kids forsook Woodstock and took a summer place out in fashionable East Hampton on Long Island. They spent the summer by the seaside. They looked for a new home in Manhattan and Dylan began the process of trying out songs for his next album, which he had decided to cut from other writers' songs.

They found the ideal property in the city, right back in the Village. A house on MacDougal Street, not much more than a stone's throw from the old West Fourth Street haunts. While the place was being fixed up they stayed out in East Hampton. The top two floors were turned into a duplex for them and the rest were let out as apartments. Bob continued to try out songs for the next album.

On July 3, the rock world was shaken by the death of Brian Jones. In 1964, when the Stones first came to New York, it had been Brian that hung out with Bob for a while. Since those days though, the blonde Stone had slipped, both creatively and personally, losing a long struggle with drugs and general desolation. Life was fragile, even at the top, you could be gone in a moment.

The Stones played in Hyde Park, London, the next day and two hundred and fifty thousand people showed up. It was the summer of monster crowds, vast rock gatherings. In the States it was Woodstock Summer, as many four hundred thousand people having been through Woodstock itself. Rock music, naked young people covered in mud, long lines for toilets, drugs, rain, abandoned automobiles, all this became a common image that summer, set beside the news from Vietnam where the war went on and on.

Bob Dylan was two hundred miles away in body and a lot further than that in spirit. In Columbia's New York studios he was putting down tracks like *King Of Fire* and *Folsom Prison Blues*, the first blocks in the building of *Self Portrait*.

But the rock festivals kept coming and Woodstock had its counterpart that summer in Britain, on the Isle of Wight. The organizers, the Foulks brothers, had been offering steadily increasing sums of money to Dylan to get him to appear. Finally at eighty thousand dollars he gave in and agreed to turn up with the Band and do a double two-and-a-half-hour set. In Europe, this news set off a pilgrimage and tens of thousands of Dylanites, who were now referred to as 'hippies', began trekking to southern England in anticipation of seeing the living legend.

In mid-July in Edwardsville, Illinois, where the Band was appearing as part of a summer tour, Bob made a surprise appearance, just for four minutes, presumably to get back the feel for playing with the Band. The Isle of Wight date was set for the end of August.

Bob went on from Illinois to Minnesota with Sara and the kids for a visit to Hibbing. Bob himself appeared at the Moose Rooms in Hibbing for a class re-union and introduced Sara to Echo Helstrom, among others. Then someone tried to pick a fight with him and he quietly slipped away.

In August, Bob and Sara flew to England. Bob looked almost plump, wore a white suit with baggy trousers and seemed utterly different from the Dylan of old. Sara was pregnant again. At the Isle of Wight Festival, Dylan was apparently awed by the size of the crowd, two hundred thousand strong.

A group of mostly American hippies had set up a camp of paper shacks that they christened *Desolation Row*. Kids from every country in Europe and beyond were there.

Dylan had told reporters beforehand that he intended to do a three-hour set, but when he finally appeared, at eleven on Sunday night, he played for just one hour. He was nervous and in a hurry to get through his songs, throwing them off with as little feeling, as if he was a cabaret artist shuffling through some old standards in a supper club. The audience which, by that time, would've applauded a dead chicken if it were called Dylan, rose enthusiastically to everything he did, but were left puzzled and somewhat disappointed at how little they'd received for their days of waiting in the mud.

While in Britain, Dylan stayed with the Harrisons and also visited John Lennon. Beatles and Stones galore turned up at the Isle of Wight, something that took a helicopter ride to achieve by Sunday, the press were there in droves. On his way out of England, Bob told a reporter that he didn't think he'd come back to England again soon, "They make too much fuss about singers here."

On the Isle of Wight Bob performed seventeen songs, ranging from *Wild Mountain Thyme* to *Mighty Quinn* and *Highway 61 Revisited*. Several tracks have been released on official Dylan albums including the version of *Mighty Quinn*, which is the only recording of that song by Dylan to have been released officially and which came out on another 'best of' compilation LP, *Bob Dylan's Greatest Hits Vol II*. In addition, most of the other songs were bootlegged in various guises under such titles as *Isle Of Wight*.

Back in the US, Bob and Sara moved into their new home in the Village and returned to the quiet life. Sara soon gave birth to Samuel, their fifth and final child. Dylan took time to seek out a good school in the neighborhood for Maria, and later Jesse to attend.

On October 21, Jack Kerouac died and for a moment there was sadness throughout the youth culture; Kerouac had been a trail-blazer for much of the rock generation's experiences and insights.

In November, Rolling Stone Magazine published an interview recorded with Jann Wenner in June. Bob had only agreed to the interview after a great deal of hesitation. In 1968, Rolling Stone had selected Dylan as their choice for President of the USA. In this lengthy interview, Dylan seemed evasive and even a little simple-minded (or uninterested) concerning the problems of the world. The impression was left of a person who just wrote his songs, who wasn't terribly worried about the rest of the world and didn't know much about it anyway. The interview had a telling effect throughout the 'movement' and many finally gave up their feeling that Dylan was in any way a figurehead for a philosophy, or even someone who really did know what was going on.

Dylan returned to the self-imposed retreat from the media that he'd come to prefer. Nothing more was heard about him until the following spring. During this time, he recorded a great number of songs, all by other writers, songs like Paul Simon's *The Boxer*. By the spring of 1970 there was a rumor about Bob Dylan's new album. It was called *Blue Moon* and featured other artists' songs. Then it appeared, called *Self Portrait* and decorated with a harshly primitive Dylan painting of himself.

*Self Portrait* was a stunner; nobody really knew what to make of it. Critics foamed and wept; it was so lamentable, it was laughable. Many who bought it found it hard to listen to. Essentially Bob had forgotten his strong suit, which is the singing of his own songs, and had continued out on the "product" limb. Maybe he thought this was the way he had to go, like Elvis and the other earlier stars, doing 'specialty' LPs, 'gospel' LPs, who knows... even 'Bob Dylan Sings Oklahoma'-type albums.

Anomaly or not, *Self Portrait* continued Dylan's very respectable sales figures, reaching No. 4 in the album charts. A single called *Wig Wam* backed by *Copper Kettle* got to No. 44 and received some airplay.

Dylan was apparently rather surprised by the vehemence of the rejection of *Self Portrait*. It was a project that he'd worked on for more than a year and it seems he simply wasn't expecting the fierce criticism he received. However, in this area, it must be said that he himself had set their standards several years before, and *Self Portrait* just didn't make it.

He was back in the studio soon afterwards. In September he cut songs for another album, to be titled *New Morning*. When quizzed about the speed with which he moved to record *New Morning* by Larry Sloman some years later, Dylan denied that it was due to the poor reception given to *Self Portrait*:

No that's wrong. We had a few of the tracks for *New Morning* before that *Self Portrait* LP came out. I didn't say, "Oh, my God, they don't like this! Let me do another one." It wasn't like that. It just happened coincidentally that one came out and the other did as soon as it did.

While Dylan was putting finishing touches to *New Morning*, there came further reminders of the fragility of rock stardom. On September 18, Jimi Hendrix died in London from inhalation of vomit under the influence of drugs. On October 4, Janis Joplin died in L.A. from an overdose. The loneliness and the boredom, the general weirdness of the life and the touring drove them to drugs and drink and had become a virtual cliché of Rock 'n' Roll: You could be rich, famous and stone miserable.

*New Morning* came out a couple of weeks later and received a rather gentle reception from the critics. Perhaps they'd exhausted the vitriol reserves over *Self Portrait*, or perhaps they were just relieved to have the real Bob Dylan to kick around again. However, the warmth of the welcome back was muted a little by the fact that *New Morning* was pretty limited stuff, compared to the old Dylan. Here were happy songs, celebrating the joys of the country life, clean air, a lovely wife, music of contentment, not what people were used to from Bob Dylan.

119

*If Not For You* was clearly dedicated to Sara. Bob was making it public – Sara had rescued him from the lonely horror of being a Rock Star that no one could talk to, except to flatter. *Day Of The Locusts* dealt with Bob's big moment at Princeton University that summer when he was awarded an honorary doctorate "as one of the most creative popular musicians of the last decade." *If Dogs Run Free* had Dylan singing in a kind of jazz-scat style, while *Father Of Night* reaffirmed again Dylan's religious convictions. Perhaps *Went To See The Gypsy* was the stand-out cut on the album. All in all, however, the music on *New Morning* was generally slight and the songs offered little to the legions of fans nurtured on stronger Dylan material.

Still *New Morning* sold respectably, reaching No. 7 in the US album chart.

Bob Dylan seemed to have lost interest in making music for a while. Possibly the ugly reception given *Self Portrait* had soured him on the whole business, or perhaps it was that in his happiness, he just didn't find many things that excited him to write songs, or perhaps it was that what songs he was writing he knew were of limited appeal. Either way, he was not to cut another album – outside of the soundtrack for *Pat Garrett & Billy The Kid* – for three years.

There were other things for him to do. His family was growing up. He set out to rediscover his roots as a Jew. In 1971 and 1972 he travelled to Israel a number of times. He studied Hebrew and the Talmud. In Israel he found something that many Jews from the diaspora have found – a powerful almost mystical sense of purpose. He was impressed by this, he made donations to Israeli Kibbutzim and in the USA visited the Jewish Defense League a few times. He investigated the message of militant Jewishness preached by Rabbi Meir Kahane (also from Minnesota) built on the powerful slogan "Never Again".

In 1971 therefore, the only Dylan records to appear were a couple of singles and another greatest hits album. Early in the year came *Watching The River Flow* backed by *Spanish Is The Loving Tongue*, but this aroused little chart interest. Later in the year Bob collaborated vigorously with Columbia in selecting material for *Bob Dylan's Greatest Hits Vol II*. (In UK – *More Bob Dylan Greatest Hits*.) In October he and Happy Traum recorded three of the songs from the Basement Tapes, at the time still only available on bootlegs, *Down In The Flood*, *I Shall Be Released* and *You Ain't Goin' Nowhere*. The album also contained a live version of *Mighty Quinn* recorded at the Isle of Wight. It was a big seller, reaching No. 10 in the album charts, despite being a full-priced double record set and a greatest hits album.

Then there was *George Jackson*, a surprisingly angry little single that Bob felt impelled to record after the death of Jackson, a black leader in the movement for prisoners' rights, gunned down by prison guards in California's Soledad Prison. The anger and bitterness in *George Jackson* reminded many of the old Dylan, the Dylan of *Who Killed Davey Moore* and the other 'finger pointing' songs. It contributed to the mystification of many who wondered why Dylan would let something like the unjust death of George Jackson move him enough to put out a single, while remaining immune to the ongoing horror in Vietnam, or the multitude of other blatant injustices happening every day inside the USA.

His only public performance in 1971 came when George Harrison persuaded him to turn up for the Bangladesh Benefit Concert on August 1. Bob appeared in both the first and the second shows. The second was released by Apple Records as an official album. The first has been bootlegged, and the chief difference between the sets is that, in the first, Bob sang *Love Minus Zero No Limit* in addition to *Hard Rain*, *Blowin' In The Wind*, *Just Like A Woman* and *It Takes A Lot To Laugh, It Takes A Train To Cry*. In the second set he sang *Mr. Tambourine Man* instead. Both performances were good and Bob sang the old songs with something like his old spirit.

Towards the end of the year, there was another sad note in the rock 'n' roll dirge of early deaths. Edie Sedgwick, one time Queen of the Scene in New York during Dylan's ascendance, died of an overdose of drugs in California. That summer of course Jim Morrison had also been found dead of a heart attack in Paris, France.

Another rare public appearance by Dylan came at the end of the year at the Band's New Year's Eve Concert at Carnegie Hall, which was recorded and eventually released as the double album *Rock Of Ages*. Dylan was seen to be cheerful, in good spirits and relaxed.

And *relaxed* described 1972, as far as Dylan fans were concerned. Bob released no records at all during the year.

He was not entirely at a loose end however, as in the summer Sam Peckinpah hired him to produce the soundtrack music for his new film *Pat Garrett & Billy The Kid*. Dylan also got a bit part in the movie, playing a character called no more than Alias. Bob did have a few lines, carried a knife, gave cryptic messages, but as he said of it:

> I don't know who I played. I tried to play whoever it was

in the story, but I guess it's a known fact that there was nobody in that story that was the character I played.

However, Bob put a lot of energy into the soundtrack, and though the versions of the songs that were released on the album *Pat Garrett & Billy The Kid* are not the same as those in the movie, they are similar. Dylan recorded them all several times and did a commendable job; the movie was a romantic Western and the brooding music he came up with served it very well. There exists a bootleg tape, just a fragment, of the actual film music and there is said to be other tapes of more versions of *Billy* and *Turkey In The Straw*.

While he was working on the movie, Dylan was living in Southern California. He decided he liked the life there and so the family moved out of Manhattan and into Malibu.

Dylan also became good friends with Kris Kristofferson who played Billy.

The movie and the album came out in 1973. Neither got rave reviews – the movie was a little unreal and the album didn't seem to please the rock-hungry reviewing corps. However, the songs have stood the test of time pretty well, and they certainly conveyed a powerful sense of the romance of Billy The Kid.

It was recorded by MGM who then sold it to Columbia. Since Dylan had been negotiating for a new contract with other companies, he was less than pleased to see Columbia continue its string of Dylan releases, even when he wasn't under contract to them. Whatever he did, they would always own him, which seemed to be the unwritten rule. This experience, when added to his memories of the hassles of 1967, were to drive him to David Geffen's aptly-named new label, Asylum, which was in the vanguard of new labels putting out the singer-songwriter sound of Los Angeles in the mid-seventies.

The experience however, was something that Bob carefully laid away. In an interview with Mary Travers in Montreal in 1974, Dylan discussed his experience in making this film, and how it had affected his own film making plans. Dylan:

> I'm not a movie star, but I've got a vision to put up on the screen. Someday we'll get around to doing it. The Peckinpah experience was valuable in terms of getting near the big action.
>
> The Peckinpah movie brought me as close as I'll get. I've been on movie sets and TV shows but they were small-time compared. They spent four-five million on *Billy The Kid*, had all the top people. So that was really heavy, Gave me that vibration.

The soundtrack album did very well for Bob; *Pat Garrett & Billy The Kid* reached No. 16 in the US album chart, and the single *Knockin' On Heaven's Door* reached No. 12 and got considerable airplay during the summer.

Despite the layoff and the relative paucity of new material that Dylan had produced since '68, his audience was still there, had grown steadily year after year. His career had languished somewhat and the release of *Self Portrait* had been a major error perhaps, but they were still out there waiting to see Bob Dylan again, and he was getting interested in being seen once more.

# CHAPTER NINE

# Blood On The Tracks

**B**y summer 1973, Dylan was getting seriously restless. It was seven years since his motorcycle accident, seven years since he'd toured. It was time to go back out and do the thing that he admits he knows the best. Maybe the happy homelife was finally getting to be a little claustrophobic.

Whatever the reasons, Bob was busy negotiating with Bill Graham a tour of the US with the Band, to run through early '74. He was also shopping for a new record company, and this time, he himself held most of the cards. Columbia had been less than wonderful to him on a few occasions. The memory of '66/'67 was sharp and clear, reinforced by the maneuvers over *Pat Garrett & Billy The Kid*.

David Geffen offered a short term contract, good money up front. Geffen like many others, had been expecting this move from Dylan. The thinking being that after being holed up for seven years, Dylan was likely to explode at some point soon. Geffen offered a small, sympathetic record company instead of a corporate monster that would damage an artist without hardly thinking about it in the search for the bottom line.

Dylan signed to Asylum and at the end of the year, with the tour of the Band lined up – twenty-six cities, big theatres, auditoriums – it was decided it would be a good idea to have a new record out, and fast.

Bob went into the studio in L.A. with the Band. Dylan has rarely worried too much about 'perfect' takes, 'perfect' sound or heavy studio work, being allied to the spirit of rock 'n' roll rather than the mechanic. Thus *Planet Waves*, his first album of new material since *New Morning* in 1970, was recorded in three days. Robbie Robertson said of this session that:

> *Planet Waves* was as good as we could make it in the situation. Under the circumstances, I thought it was extraordinary. There were a lot of simple songs on that

album and people didn't necessarily want to hear very simple songs from him. I mean every once in a while they take a *Knockin' On Heaven's Door* just to kind of get on with it, but basically what they want is a complex song...

The tour planning went on. To take up the business heat and to act as liaison between the Graham people and himself, Bob called on an old Minnesota buddy named Lou Kemp. Kemp was a good businessman – a millionaire fish processor – and he was to become an important factor in the success of the Rolling Thunder Tour in 1975.

For the '74 tour, there was considerable excitement in all twenty-six selected tour cities. The first Dylan tour in aeons, zonks, etc., the lines formed early and the shows sold out, fast.

*Planet Waves* was duly released, to mild critical applause. It was a nice record, although obviously put together very quickly. It featured few too many cheerful songs of family life for the critics' tastes. To some, it was grotesque to hear Dylan attempting to reconcile his wild, artistic vision with domestic bliss. To others, it seemed miraculously lively. It sold briskly enough anyway, and during the tour itself, in February '74, it was at No. 1 in the US charts.

A single *On A Night Like This* was to reach No. 44 at the same time. Before *Planet Waves* however, there had appeared a singular piece of corporate revenge. Columbia had rushed out a compilation album called *Dylan* in time for Christmas. It was essentially a set of out-takes from the *Self Portrait* sessions and contained some lamentable stuff, including an all too funny version of Joni Mitchell's *Big Yellow Taxi*. *Dylan* however still reached No. 17 in the charts and sold pretty well.

The tour kicked off in the New Year, in Chicago, on January 3. Rock media from most of the civilized world was in attendance. This was the hottest ticket of the season. The Chicago shows were also very good, so it is said. Dylan and the Band were tight and the audience wore itself out. From Chicago they moved onto the East Coast, ranged up to Canada, then down to Miami before going back out to the Mid-West and finishing off January in New York. Then back across the country to California, ending the tour at the Forum in L.A.

The Graham people knew their stuff; the tour went like clockwork. Of this, Dylan was later to complain to Ratso Slocum:

> I wasn't really in control of the situation. Nobody was in control. We were just shuffled around from airport to

limo to hotel lobby, to hockey rinks. I felt like Willis Reed (pro-basketball star). And in order for me to do whatever it is that I do, I have to have control and I didn't have too much control on that specific tour...

The set didn't change much throughout. They stuck to the same pattern, starting with *Most Likely You'll Go Your Way* and carrying on with *Lay Lady Lay, Just Like Tom Thumb's Blues, I Don't Believe You, It Ain't Me Babe, Ballad Of A Thin Man, All Along The Watchtower, Hollis Brown, Knockin' On Heaven's Door, The Times Are A Changing, Gates Of Eden, It's Alright Ma, Don't Think Twice, Forever Young, Something There Is About You, Like A Rolling Stone* and ended on a reprise of *Most Likely You'll Go Your Way*.

At first, Dylan refused to do encores it is said. He felt that it was just a crowd ritual, but then one night Graham turned the house lights up at the end so Dylan could see the crowd. Dylan did encores after that.

There were a few variations on the set; a new song, not included on *Planet Waves* called *Except You*, was played at a few shows, including Chicago. In St. Louis there was *Desolation Row*, *Visions Of Johanna* appeared in Denver, and *Blowin' In The Wind* at a few places.

Critics covering the tour agreed broadly that Dylan seemed uptight, and the pretty drastic reinterpretations of his old material were wrenching for a lot of people who'd been listening to those old records for years. *It's Alright Ma* this time around was a rocker for instance – the lyrics jammed up and dispensed with minimum feeling.

This criticism spilled over to the double album taken live from the tour, *Before The Flood*. This reached No. 3 in the US. Dylan sounds in a hurry to get through each song and the Band sound as competent as ever.

Another aspect of this tour was that this was the one that produced a billion bootlegs. First off there were the *White Bear* boots, eighteen double albums, all put out within a month of the tour. They were well recorded and are said to have come from tapes taken directly from the PA systems.

Exactly who it was that managed to produce such a volume of bootleg tape from such a well organized tour remains a mystery.

In addition, there were hundreds of audience tapes, from which there are many, many boots. For the most part, these are easily ignored by collectors – there is, after all, already a live album.

The tour over and with *Planet Waves* a triumphant No. 1, despite the critics somewhat cool response, Bob tripped back to Los Angeles riding high.

He found that the problems in his marriage were getting serious; a split came, and they seperated – he moving out to new quarters in L.A. and she staying in Malibu.

In May he turned up to perform at the Friends of Chile Benefit and did four numbers, *Spanish Is The Loving Tongue*, *Blowin' In The Wind*, *North Country Blues* – on his own – and *Deportees* – with Arlo Guthrie. He also got very drunk and legend has it, fell off the stage.

Through the summer of '74, Bob continued to write new songs, songs filled with pain and doubt – the legacy of his separation from Sara. A new album was already taking shape.

He left Asylum and David Geffen too, and re-signed with Columbia once more. In the autumn he went to New York and started recording the new songs. Phil Ramone was producing and John Hammond Sr. was there in the studio, to see the prodigal back home once more.

There was a problem though in getting the studio musicians they'd wanted, so Bob called up friends on the folk music grapevine and filled the studio with folkies, among them Buddy Cage, Eric Weissberg and Barry Kornfeld.

The songs for what was to be *Blood On The Tracks* were soon recorded. However, five of the original recordings were later re-mixed, although a few copies of the 'original' *Blood On The Tracks* escaped the net and, of course, spawned a host of boots. The five re-recorded songs were *If You See Her Say Hello*, and *Lily, Rosemary And The Jack Of Hearts*, *Tangled Up In Blue*, *You're A Big Girl Now* and *Idiot Wind*. The first time around these were simpler – the tunes less developed – with just acoustic guitar and bass accompaniment. *Idiot Wind* in particular, changed considerably the second time around, plus there are lyrical differences between the first and second version of *Tangled Up In Blue*. The song's story begins in the third person instead of being told in the first person, for example.

Among the bootlegs carrying the five original cuts is a very rare one, called *Joaquin Antique*, which was withdrawn early on because of a persistent jump on the record during *Idiot Wind*. Rarity has naturally driven its price sky high – a mint copy with original cover (unplayed) is perhaps the most valuable of all Dylan boots.

The same five tracks can also be found on others, like *Pass Over & Rolling Thunder*.

127

Once the changes had been made, the result, *Blood On The Tracks*, as most of us know it, was released towards the end of the year and reached No. 1 in the US album chart by February '75. *Blood On The Tracks* marked a solid resurgence in Dylan's standing with the critics. Here was Dylan brought down from the cloud castles of his wealth and his happy family life; now it was easier to relate to him. Dylan, caught up in the toils of a disintegrating marriage which had spanned eight years and five kids, was not a cheerful fellow. Neither was this music the brilliant madness of *Blonde On Blonde,* nor the almost accidental glory of *Highway 61 Revisited* – there are no Mike Bloomfields, Al Koopers or Charlie McCoys on hand this time to lift the musical end of things. The major failing of the album is the rather slight quality of the actual playing but, as ever, Bob sought spontaneity in the studio.

Nevertheless, the critics generally liked it; there were some raves, it sold well and it presented a very new version of Bob Dylan. This was an older Dylan, sadder and wiser, and bearing considerable pain. The sadness of *Blood On The Tracks* is evident: "I'm Going Out Of My Mind with a cork screw in through my heart... since we've been apart...." In September '75, Bob commented on the reaction to *Blood On The Tracks*:

> A lot of people tell me they enjoy that album. It's hard for
> me to relate to that, I mean it, you know, people
> enjoying that type of pain, you know?

Undoubtedly, life had gotten serious for Bob Dylan – some old tendencies were reinforced and others faded away. With a song like *Idiot Wind*, he effectively used the old scathing invective to trump *Positively 4th Street* with infinite corners of accusation. This was a mature mind at work, dealing with serious hurt. But the old Dylan humor was gone and there would be no more *115th Dreams, I Shall Be Free No. 10* or even anything like *Rainy Day Women Nos. 12 & 35*.

*Blood On The Tracks* however, remained an important boost to Dylan's credibility. Throughout the seventies he'd enjoyed consistent chart success; now he'd come up with another album to stand beside *John Wesley Harding* and the other great ones from the sixties. *Blood On The Tracks* measured up well and this critical success confirmed him in the direction he'd set out on in '74. Rock 'n' roll was what he did, that was his trade, and therefore he must go out and get back to it. He also wanted to try and find a way to take the grief out of touring.

Taking the grief out of touring has become almost a quest for the holy grail in older, still active rock groups. Going night after night, place to place, jet plane to jet plane, can be an exhausting, alienating experience at the very least. It's a young person's game – OK when you're twenty three and ready to take on the world full throttle but by the age of thirty five, it is generally one unmitigated horror. Dylan pondered the idea of a band-o'-gypsies style tour. Loose, musicians coming and going, friends dropping by for a bit, doing small clubs and halls. Possibly not even a national tour, just do one region at a time, one or two a year.

In late March, Bob turned up for the S.N.A.C.K. benefit broadcast on FM radio. Also there were Garth Hudson, Levon Helm and Rick Danko from the Band, Neil Young, Tim Drummond and Ben Keith. They did nine songs, ranging from *The Weight* to a medley of *Helpless* and *Knockin' On Heaven's Door*. Of course, a bootleg exists, called *S.N.A.C.K.*, and apparently it is an audience tape rather than a nice FM recording off a good radio receiver, yet another oddity of the bootlegger's market.

In April, Dylan took off for a vacation, visiting France and Corsica. While there, he decided to try and set up a 'band-o'-gypsies'-type tour. Humanscale, loose personnel, he'd just call up his friends and see who wanted to go out on the road. They'd go by bus, do small halls and clubs. It would be enjoyable work, which musicians like himself could get off on.

Back in New York, he agreed to let Columbia put out *The Basement Tapes*, which appeared shortly afterwards. At last, these great songs were released to a wider public than the bootleg market. The two record set soon moved up the charts, hitting No. 7. This, despite seven years of intensive bootlegging of those songs. Of course, mysteries remained: why did they leave off *Mighty Quinn*? Were there other songs that have never been booted and were also left off here? Dylanophilia is full of such areas of theory and wishful thinking.

Bob had also found a cause to get angry about. He'd read a book sent to him by Rubin Carter, the black ex-middleweight champion of the world, who'd been jailed in 1967, convicted on slim evidence of the killing of two whites in a bar hold-up in '66. An all-white New Jersey jury had sent him away for life and by 1974, he was in Trenton State Prison. Dylan had got the book while he was in California and the mad injustice of what had been done stayed with him. When he got back to the East Coast, he went out and visited "Hurricane" Carter, who'd been rotting in state prisons for eight years. Dylan took up Hurricane's cause, and pledged himself to try and get him a re-trial. For a star like Dylan obviously the best method was to write a song, and then do a benefit concert.

Back on the streets of the Village again, Bob was seen in all the old haunts. He ran into Jacques Levy, who'd written many songs for Roger McGuinn, and did some directing on Broadway. Dylan and Levy got to drinking together and Bob told him he had some new songs but he needed to get some more work done on them. One thing led to another and they went round the corner of Levy's place and Dylan played an early version of *Isis*. They began to work on it together. Things continued to go well, so Dylan suggested they get out of the City – it was summer anyway – and go out to East Hampton, which he knew well.

In East Hampton they worked on the rest of the songs on the album, except *One More Cup Of Coffee*, which Bob already had and *Sara* which he wrote by himself.

Towards the end of July they came back to the city and Bob immediately began planning a recording session. As always, he needed some musicians and he started searching the bars, venues and even the streets.

He dropped in on Jack Elliott, during Jack's set at the Other End. Bob got up on stage with Elliott and they did a duet of *Pretty Boy Floyd*, one for the old days. Then Bob sang a new song, and created another Dylan mystery-cum-controversy. The song was *St. John The Evengelist*, which sounded lyrically and musically like something from *Blonde On Blonde*. Dylan was never to record it officially and thus it exists only on an audience tape bootleg from that one Jack Elliott concert. An EP called *Valentino Type Tango* carries the song.

On July 28, Dylan assembled a small army of musicians and friends in Columbia's New York studio. Emmylou Harris was there, Eric Clapton too and an eight-piece English rhythm 'n' blues outfit called Kokomo. There were several studio musicians; there was Bob Neuwirth and a lady with a violin called Scarlett Rivera, who Dylan had found on a street corner in the East Village. It was another memorable and chaotic Dylan recording session.

The first night, they made it through six or seven songs including a version of *Durango* with Clapton on guitar, that survived to get on the eventual album. They also jumped from one thing to another a lot. Clapton said it was "madness". Other songs dealt with included *Catfish* – Dylan's ode to 'Catfish' Hunter, pitching star for the Oakland As – *Mozambique, Oh Sister*, plus a couple of songs that never made it to the record,

*Wire Tapping* and *Money Blues*. There was also a long version of *Hurricane* with virtually a disco beat.

Clapton described the scene to a Rolling Stone Magazine interviewer:

> That was amazing. He was trying to find a situation you see where he could make music with new people. He was just driving around, picking up musicians and bringing them back to the sessions. It ended up with something like twenty four musicians in the studio, all playing these incredibly incongruous instruments.

Inevitably, this first session became an exploratory one. A few nights later though, with just five musicians and Bob, a lot of songs were laid down. For this session there was Rob Stoner on bass; Howie Wyeth on drums; a lady named Sheena, a singer-songwriter who'd known Dylan since the sixties and Scarlett Rivera and her violin. From this session came *One More Cup Of Coffee, Joey, Oh Sister, Black Diamond Bay, Mozambique* and *Hurricane*.

They also cut *Rita Mae*, a song which was kept off the album but which was later released as the B side of a single in '77, backing a live version of *Memphis Blues Again*.

Also present that night in the studio was Sara Dylan, being very quiet and seemingly not terribly impressed with what was happening. She'd seen it all before of course, but she was there because Bob and herself were making up.

Over the next few days the recording group parted, while Dylan and Neuwirth listened to the tapes carefully. Now Bob was talking about his idea for a loose, small scale tour. He was calling it things like 'The Montezuma Review' and 'The Rolling Thunder Review'. Old friends and new recording group alike were enthusiastic about the idea.

However, when Columbia was approached and asked if they'd like to back the 'Rolling Thunder Review', the response was decisively negative.

Undaunted, Dylan continued to plan. With the new album entitled *Desire* finished, Sara and himself took off to Minnesota for a spell. Bob called on Lou Kemp again; this time he wanted Lou to serve as full tour organizer. Kemp agreed and soon Bob started making calls across the nation, reeling in the stars.

Now that the Rolling Thunder Tour was fitting together, Bob started the wheels turning on the other half of his grand scheme. This was the film he had always wanted to do, where they would create characters out of the people in the tour, where they'd mix fact footage with fantasy, to probe the questions of identity, of anomie, of loss and life and love. The whole thing to be created from the side-swash of a rock 'n' roll tour.

Howard Alk, who had worked on the aborted *Eat The Document* nine years before, was back. Cameras and cameramen were hired.

In September, there came a call for Dylan to perform on the John Hammond TV Special being recorded for PBS in Chicago. Dylan took along Stoner, Wyeth and Rivera and turned up looking wild and shaggy wearing a pair of black and white striped trousers. He did *Oh Sister* (with a dig at Baez) plus *Simple Twist Of Fate* and he revealed *Hurricane* to the world. It was a pretty good performance, and of course it was bootlegged. The results can be found on records like *Passed Over & Rolling Thunder*, and *Blood Takes*.

Columbia released *Hurricane* as the next Dylan single and it gained considerable airplay, considering that it was a protest song so far out of its time. On a singles chart dominated by disco however, it was not a commercial record. It reached No. 33 for a week or two and then slipped away.

The filming began in New York, scenes with David Blue in the Village, talking about the old days, when Dylan was on the streets, in the hoots and bars. Alk and Dylan now controlled "the eye"; they worked loosely, filming everywhere, at parties, offices, hotel rooms. Throughout the tour there would be constant scene creation and shooting. Sam Shepherd, the playwright, was asked to come and write screenplay material.

A tribe was gathering for the tour as well. Joan Baez had cancelled some dates of her own and was coming. Allen Ginsberg was coming, there was to be a visit to Kerouac's grave and a sunrise ceremony. Joni Mitchell was due. Roger McGuinn, the ex-Byrd was there and so was Jack Elliott and Mick Ronson, ex-guitarist with Bowie. Ronnee Blakeley, Bob Neuwirth, and newly- christened "Guam", the band of Stoner, Wyeth and Rivera.

Joan Baez had a few initial fears, which she later told Larry Slocum about. "I just thought it was very exciting, kind of nerve-racking. I didn't trust a lot of it. I said, What if Ramblin' Jack Elliott decides he wants to leave on a freight train for two months and Bobby Neuwirth decides to throw himself in the ocean? I mean what's that leave? ('Cause I've known these guys for a long time and I love them dearly, but everybody's a little unstable.)"

This first outing of the Rolling Thunder Review was in the direction of New England. They were to wind their way through

Massachusetts to Maine and then across the border to Canada for gigs in Quebec, Montreal and Toronto. Then it'd be time to get down to New York for the Madison Square Concert – a benefit for Rubin Carter's Defense Fund on December 8.

The first gig was in Plymouth, Massachusetts and, true to the advance hype, it was to a small place. However, as the tour went on, the gigs got bigger and the Canadian ones would be in auditoriums. There were implications here that because the tour had been set up to do small halls and clubs with the musicians just getting musician's scale pay, that Dylan would lose money on the venture. Trucking forty people around plus a film crew for a few weeks costs plenty.

There were also visits to places like Kerouac's grave, where Dylan and Ginsberg improvised a scene for the cameras. Ginsberg read a poem, improvised another; Dylan played harmonium and guitar, did a blues.

The energy was high; Dylan was enjoying it. Sara was with him and she was also taking part in the film. There were many scenes shot with her, Baez and Dylan together, plus there were the gigs which were enjoyable too.

Generally speaking, the Rolling Thunder set at these shows began with a Joni Mitchell set. Others would do spots and then Baez would come on, followed by Dylan – his set beginning with *When I Paint My Masterpiece*, and running on with *It Ain't Me Babe, Hard Rain, Durango, Isis, I Shall Be Released, One More Cup Of Coffee, Oh Sister, Hurricane, Sara* and *Just Like A Woman*, before finishing on *Knockin' On Heaven's Door*. There were plenty of variations though and many can be found on audience tapes and bootlegs derived from them.

It seems that nearly everyone enjoyed themselves, although Joni Mitchell had a terrible cold that wouldn't go away, but the relentless pressures of the usual sort of touring were absent. It wasn't plane, airport, hotel room at least, although everyone was giving their services pretty cheaply.

The filming went on and the inter-linked scenes of, what was to become Dylan's film, *Renaldo And Clara* were shot on this first leg of the tour.

After the Canadian concerts they headed down to New York. First there was a gig out in the prison in New Jersey for Rubin Carter and the inmates. The inmate population was heavily black and they didn't really respond too well to Joni Mitchell, or indeed to much of the set. There has yet to surface an audience tape or a bootleg of this particular gig – a surprising omission perhaps.

At the Madison Square Garden gig there was tons of press, pressure and politicking. Speeches were made, some speakers hardly mentioning Rubin Carter. The show rolled, a good one by all accounts and that was that for the first stage of the Rolling Thunder Revue.

Baez and Joni Mitchell split for California. The rest of the group broke up for Christmas.

Dylan and family stayed in New York. In January *Desire* was released to generally favorable reviews. It swiftly became Dylan's best ever selling album, his second Gold record and another No. 1. *Hurricane* was all over the FM radio, along with *Sara* and *Joey*. A whole new audience, a young one, that had never been interested in Dylan before, now began to pick up on him.

Soon afterwards the Rolling Thunder Review formed, but now without Joni Mitchell. The tour rolled south this time and then westwards, playing a few large places as well as some small halls. Things finally ground to a halt on May 23 with the recording of the Rolling Thunder TV Special. Afterwards, they held a memorable party, for Dylan's thirty fifth birthday.

A live album was later released, called *Hard Rain* with a representative set. Innumerable audience tapes and bootlegs exist and there is a bootleg known as *Bridgett's Album – A Vinyl Headstone Almost In Place*, which has the songs from the TV special that weren't included on *Hard Rain*.

*Desire* was another very good album for Bob with the critics, and it certainly was a hit with the fans. Dylan's reputation had risen once more. On *Desire*, the complex songs like *Isis* were complemented by the love songs like *Sara* and the topical songs like *Hurricane*. There was even the ironic little rocker *Mozambique*. However, once again, the album suffers from the lack of a really great band.

While the Rolling Thunder tour was moving across the mid-west in March, Rubin Carter won release from prison pending a new trial, scheduled for that December.

# CHAPTER TEN

## Renaldo & Clara

If the years 1967-73 had been relatively fallow ones for Dylan, the two and a half years that followed the recording of *Planet Waves* were tremendously active. The Rolling Thunder Review and the success of *Desire* marked a tremendous recovery in his career. Furthermore, *Blood On The Tracks* had regained him the respect of the critics, something easily lost but not so readily won back.

Thus, Dylan had re-emerged from the pleasant semi-obscurity of his Point Dume, Malibu estate and quickly won back the position he had held before the motorcycle accident of 1966. Or almost – since this was a mature Dylan, the father of five kids, a man who'd lost the blush of adolescence, even of youth, that had been a part of his image in the sixties. But his audience had grown older too and brought their own children into the world and experienced all the other pains of growing up; in truth, everyone had spilt a little blood on the tracks.

And if, as it seemed, it took a restless, unhappy Bob Dylan to create great songs again, then to his fans and the critics this was acceptable. Of course Dylan himself found this aspect of his regained career a little hard to take; he expressed his revulsion at it, but this was an aspect that he'd had to face since the sixties and to that extent things hadn't changed. The fact remained that a happily married Dylan, living out of public view with his family, was a Dylan that came up with precious little in the way of good songs.

Now in mid-'76 he was due for a rest, having completed two major tours of the USA and three albums of new songs, two live albums and *The Basement Tapes* from '67.

Reconciled with Sara since the previous July, Bob returned with her to Malibu. He spent the summer there and little was heard from the Dylan entourage.

In the fall, on October 25, he travelled up to San Francisco to join the Band for *The Last Waltz*, a grand show at Winterland that was filmed by Martin Scorsese and recorded as well. This was the Band's farewell performance after a career that had began in the late fifties.

Dylan did six songs in the show, of which three were to appear on the *The Last Waltz* album. All six have shown up on a collector's tape in addition and may have been bootlegged too. They were *Baby Let Me Follow You Down, Hazel, I Don't Believe You, Forever Young*, a reprise of *Baby Let Me Follow You Down* and *I Shall Be Released*. The last, which wasn't put on the official album had all the other performers present singing along on the chorus.

In general, Dylan and the Band sounded pretty much the same here as they had in '74 except that the Band's sound was heavier and more attention was given to actually following the tunes. *Forever Young* was perhaps the best cut and the one with the tune mostly intact. Dylan, however, throws off the lines in some songs in the same drastic way he had in '74.

Following *The Last Waltz*, Dylan went back to Malibu. His next project, and probably the most demanding of his career, was the fashioning of the film footage that had been shot during the first leg of the Rolling Thunder tour in late '75. It is clear that Bob had a serious hankering for film-making – he'd wanted to make a movie for years. He now got down to the serious task of editing, cutting and splicing together the many hours of footage that had accumulated during the Rolling Thunder tour, with the object of producing the film he had always intended to make.

In December '76, there came the saddening news that Hurricane Carter's retrial had gone badly. Without the aid of any new evidence, and with the testimony of the same witnesses unshaken, Carter and John Artis wound up losing their re-trial and were sent back to prison.

Bob continued work on his film but, as 1977 rolled on, gossip concern in his marriage surfaced once more. The troubles grew and by March 1, Sara was in court in Santa Monica, California, seeking a divorce. The petition for divorce stated that the "respondent, Robert Dylan, is hereby restrained and enjoined from harassing, annoying, molesting or in any way interfering with the peace and quiet and personal privacy of the petitioner, Sara Dylan." Sara also sought exclusive use of the couple's house in Malibu and temporary custody of their five children.

A couple of weeks later, Dylan was in court himself and the divorce proceedings went through quickly. Since California is a "communal property" state, all the Dylan's assets, including the Malibu complex, property in East Hampton, Woodstock and New York City, and elsewhere were involved.

Within weeks they were divorced and it was over – the marriage that had saved Bob Dylan from the craziness of 1966 and removed him from the rock scene, at the time when his influence and prestige were at their greatest. He was on his own once more.

Dylan threw himself into his work on the film, a title for which had now appeared, it was to be called *Renaldo & Clara*. The months went by and the film took shape and a release date was scheduled for Jan 25, 1978.

Since Dylan's energies were directed almost single-mindedly into his film project, he made no records in '76 or '77 other than the live album of the Rolling Thunder tour, *Hard Rain*. A single was released in '77 with a live version of *The Memphis Blues Again* backed by *Rita Mae*, an outtrack from the *Desire* sessions of July '75.

As the release date for *Renaldo & Clara* approached, so Bob Dylan had Paul Wasserman, who had handled publicity for him since the 1974 tour, line up interviews with the media. The first thing that Dylan told Wasserman about *Renaldo & Clara* was "It's not *Star Wars*, is it Paul?" Bob was aware that he was about to take a very risky step, leading his audience out into an area far from the comfortable rock 'n' roll arena they were used to. Into *Renaldo & Clara* he had poured a great deal of concentration, dealing with complex, difficult issues.

He told Jonathan Cott in a Rolling Stone Magazine interview in late '77:

> I'll tell you what my film is about. It's about naked
> alienation of the inner self against the outer self,
> alienation taken to the extreme. And it's about integrity.

On January 25, 1978, *Renaldo & Clara* opened simultaneously in New York and Los Angeles. There was little advertising. In Bob's words "advertising is a big thing, but we couldn't afford it, so we hired Paul." Mr. Wasserman certainly generated publicity for the film and Dylan interviews appeared in many publications, but the film itself left most critics baffled. One major complaint was that it was simply far too long at four and a quarter hours. Dylan was outraged, "I can't believe that people think that four hours is too long for a film. As if people had so much to do..." Again, to Jonathan Cott, he complained:

> I know this film is too long – I don't care. In India they
> show twelve hour movies. Americans are spoiled, they

expect art to be like wallpaper with no effort, just to be there...

The critics savaged it. In New York, the Village Voice had seven film reviewers cover it and they all tore it to pieces, primarily for self-indulgence.

When pressed by hostile interviewers, Dylan turned to the counter attack.

Q: It's not possible that the movie is at all disjointed?

Dylan: Did you sit through the whole movie?

Q: I sat through about three hours.

Dylan: Do you smoke a lot of dope?

Q: I have in my day.

Dylan: That's the reason.

Q: I'm sure there were people in the movie theatre who had smoked a lot more dope than I had.

Dylan: How old were you when you first started smoking dope?

Q: Thirteen.

Dylan: Well, O.K. There's your reason right there.

Q: Because I'm a hopeless dope addict?

Dylan: Because your mind has been... You smoked dope before you knew how to smoke dope.

*Renaldo & Clara* was edited down by Howard Alk and Bob Dylan from more than four hundred hours of film footage. This possibly explains why Bob was reluctant to cut it any further than four and a quarter hours.

The film opened with a six minute scene in which David Blue strolls around Greenwich Village and reminisces about the old days in the sixties when he first left home and ran into Dylan in New York. Thereafter, a shifting cast of the various people who were around during the Rolling Thunder Tour take up roles, sit together in restaurants and chat, give one another flowers, wear masks, ride in trains, visit a cemetery, and hold a mysterious ceremony on the edge of a distant shore where they hold hands and chant a mantra-cum-rock 'n' roll song.

The cast was made up of Bob playing Renaldo, Sara playing Clara, Ronnie Hawkins playing Bob Dylan, Joan Baez playing the mysterious Woman In White, Bob Neuwirth as the Masked Tortilla, Allen Ginsberg as The Father, Ronnee Blakely playing Mrs Bob Dylan, Jack Elliott as something called Longbeno de Castro, and Dave Blue and Roger McGuinn as themselves.

Throughout the set-up scenes, such as the bordello scene, where Joan Baez and Sara Dylan play prostitutes and Allen Ginsberg plays the john, there are intercut concert scenes of the tour itself with performances of more than forty songs, not all sung by Bob Dylan but including *When I Paint My Masterpiece, Isis, Ballad In Plain D, A Hard Rain's Gonna Fall, I Want You, It Ain't me Babe, Knocking On Heaven's Door, Hurricane, Durango, One Too Many Mornings, Sara, Sad-Eyed Lady Of The Lowlands, Tangled Up In Blue* and *Just Like A Woman.*

Four songs were released on an EP entitled: *Four Songs From Renaldo And Clara.*

Jonathan Cott asked Dylan what the relationship between the Bob Dylan in the film and Renaldo meant. Dylan said:

> There's Renaldo, there's a guy in white face singing on the stage, and then there's Ronnie Hawkins playing Bob Dylan. Bob Dylan is listed in the credits as playing Renaldo, yet Ronnie Hawkins is listed as playing Bob Dylan.

Cott: "So Bob Dylan may or may not be in the film?"
Dylan: "Exactly."
Cott: "But Bob Dylan made the film."
Dylan: "Bob Dylan didn't make it, *I* made it."

In the same interview, Dylan discussed film technique and Directors that had influenced him.

> I'm not concerned how long something is. I want to see a set shot, I *feel* a set shot. I don't feel all this motion and boom-boom. We can fast cut when we want, but the power comes in the ability to have faith that it is a meaningful shot.
>
> You know who understood this? Andy Warhol. Warhol did a lot for American cinema. He was before his time. But Warhol and Hitchcock and Peckinpah and Todd Browning, they were important to me... Godard...I never saw any film like *Breathless*...I think American film-makers are the best. But I also like Kurosawa, and my favorite director is Buñuel.

Dylan also said of the film:

> It's about the fact that you have to be faithful to your subconscious, unconscious and superconscious as well as to your conscious. Integrity is a facet of honesty. It has to do with knowing yourself...
>
> The film reveals that there's a whole lot to reveal beneath the surface of the soul, but it's unthinkable...It reveals the depths that there are to reveal. And that's the most that you can ask, because things are really very invisible. You can't reveal the invisible. And this film goes as far as we can to reveal that.

To me *Renaldo & Clara* is my first real film. I don't know who will like it. I made it for a specific bunch of people and myself and that's all. That's how I wrote *Blowin' In The Wind* and the *Times They Are A Changing*. They were written for a certain crowd of people and for certain artists too. Who knew they were going to be big songs?

In an interview with Joel Kotkin of New Times Magazine Dylan was asked:

Q: Do you care whether the movie makes money or not?

Dylan: I care, but it's not the main reason we made the movie.

Q: What would be the main reason?

Dylan: Just to get the movie out of my system.

Q: To exorcise a ghost in any way?

Dylan: No. No. It's a movie. It's an art form. I'm an artist working in art and different mediums. Who wouldn't want to make a movie if they thought they could? It's a visionary dream which I always wanted to do.

When asked by Jonathan Cott why he'd made himself so vulnerable, Dylan said:

You must be vulnerable to be sensitive to reality. And to me being vulnerable is just another way of saying that one has nothing more to lose. I don't have anything but darkness to lose. I'm way beyond that. The worst thing that could happen is that the film will be accepted and that the next one will be compared unfavorably to this one.

Dylan and Cott also discussed the Christian imagery in parts of the film and Dylan said of Jesus:

...why does Jesus really die?... Because he's a healer. Jesus is a healer. So he goes to India, finds out how to be a healer and becomes one. But see I believe that he overstepped his duties a little bit. He accepted and took on the bad karma of all the people he healed. And he was filled with so much bad karma that the only way out was to burn him up.

As it turned out, the worst thing that could happen to *Renaldo & Clara* was that it was so bad-mouthed in America by critics, who couldn't be bothered to puzzle out the layers of mystery, that hardly anybody went to see it. The criticism was relentless. Dylan had switched media and found in the Film World a level of bitchiness he had perhaps never expected. Within a few weeks *Renaldo & Clara* was withdrawn. Since Dylan had paid for it all himself, the financial hurt must have been considerable.

However, when *Renaldo & Clara* was shown at the Cannes Film Festival it received considerable praise. Too long and confusing for American tastes perhaps but not for the French and international film critics.

With his film dying at the box office, Dylan returned to the one sure thing in his life, touring. He embarked on a mammoth world tour beginning in a completely new market for him, Japan. The tour band for this trip was made up of some ex-Rolling Thunder personnel like Rob Stoner and Steve Soles, plus Ian Wallace on drums, Billy Cross on lead guitar, Dave Mansfield on pedal steel, Steve Douglas on saxophone, Alan Pasqua on keyboards, Bobbye Hall on percussion and three female singers, Helena Springs, Jo Ann Harris, and Debi Dye.

While in Japan, Dylan and the group recorded a live album *Bob Dylan At Budokan*, at the Nippon Budokan in Tokyo on February 28 and March 1. A double album set, it was released in 1979.

From Japan, Dylan went south to Australia, then moved around the world to Europe where he toured Britain once more and then Germany and France.

In Europe, the crowds came out in droves; this was the first chance they'd had to see Bob Dylan since the rather ill-fated Isle of Wight Rock Festival in 1969, almost a decade had passed and the old fans were eager to see their hero. In addition, there were new fans, younger people, who'd turned on to Dylan through hearing *Blood On The Tracks* and *Desire*.

Once back in the USA, Dylan and group embarked on a gruelling sixty-two city tour, breaking in Los Angeles to head into the studio and record a new album, *Street Legal*.

*Street Legal* was received with mixed reviews. Some critics thought it weird, others retrogressive and it was lambasted in some quarters for 'sexist' lyrics as in, "Can you cook and sew, make flowers grow" in *Is Your Love In Vain?*, and here and there it got good reviews too. The songs seem filled with mysterious imagery, some of it derived from the Tarot, and there are magicians, young witches and a rather desperate sense of longing for a woman to bring salvation perhaps, but what is missing are love songs of the calibre of *Sara* or *If You See Her Say Hello*. The themes of the album are treachery, betrayal, exile and survival and one song in particular, *No Time To Think*, opens the lid on Dylan's thoughts at this point and reveals a stark form of terror and a dreadful sense of alienation. Lines like "You know you can't keep her and the water gets deeper, and it's leading you on to the brink" and "Stripped of all virtue as you crawl through the dirt you can give but you cannot receive," leave the listener feeling a sense of desperation in Dylan that had never been there before.

In another fine interview with Jonathan Cott for Rolling Stone Magazine that was done in September '78, Dylan was asked about the many references to magic on *Street Legal*.

> These are things I'm really interested in and it's taken me a while to get back to it. Right through the time of *Blonde On Blonde* I was doing it unconsciously. Then one day I was half stepping and the lights went out. And since that point I more or less had amnesia. Now you can take that statement as literally or metaphysically as you need to, but that's what happened to me. It took me a long time to get to do consciously what I used to be able to do unconsciously.

In the same interview he said:

> I didn't create Bob Dylan. Bob Dylan has always been here... always was. When I was a child, there was Bob Dylan. And before I was born, there was Bob Dylan...

There was a sense of weariness in Dylan that was unmistakable. At one point he said to Cott:

> I've got twenty-one or twenty-three albums out on Columbia alone and about seventy-five bootleg records floating around, so it gets to a point where it doesn't matter anymore. You want each new record to be your best, but you know you're going to write more songs and make another album anyway...

This, from a man in his 37th year, embarking on a gruelling touring schedule, highlights the emptiness that now confronted him. His family life was gone, stripped away in the horror of a divorce. His hopes for a move into the film making business had been quashed, the critics calling him presumptious and egotistical for thinking he could be more than a rock singer/ songwriter. From the songs on *Street Legal* we can hear echoes of the same problems that had always afflicted him in relationships with women, at one point he even said to Cott: "I meet witchy women. Somehow I attract them. I wish they'd leave me alone." Dylan now confronted the fact that he was just doing his job and, at the end of the day, when he came home it was likely to be to an empty room somewhere, if it wasn't just an anonymous hotel room even.

# CHAPTER ELEVEN

# Born Again

The rejection of *Renaldo & Clara* left Dylan in a difficult position. First off, it came at a bad time for him in financial terms, following as it did on the heels of his divorce from Sara in a communal property state, a divorce moreover with minor children involved. He was the sole investor in *Renaldo & Clara* and therefore the sole loser financially. Even worse, it wrecked his plans for further film-making since, after such a commercial disaster, nobody in the film distribution business would give him a deal, nor could he hope to entice other financial backing. As for the major studios, any hopes he might have had in terms of interesting them in his plans for films evaporated under the harsh glare of the critical gaze.

Many observers surmised that the reason Dylan took up touring as a way of life in 1978/78 was simply because he was no longer a wealthy man and had debts. It seems incredible when one considers the royalties still accruing on all those songs, all those albums, but few things are as expensive as divorce or film-making and Bob had gone for both at the same time.

Again in terms of what he was to do next, what songs to write, what projects to get into, the failure of *Renaldo & Clara* to get much reaction from his huge audience of fans was a depressing signal. When you've been 'communicating' with millions of people for sixteen years through your work, then perhaps you come to expect them to take an interest if you put out a film. When all those legions of fans then show no interest at all it would be easy to be crushed, to want to give it all up and retire for good.

It would have been natural for Bob to question himself, to begin to wonder if he really had lost it and to lose the will power to go on. After all, what Dylan has done for a career is something that few people have ever done, to not only get on a stage before thousands and thousands and knock 'em dead with rock 'n' roll, but to do it with your very own songs, year after year after year. That takes will power and determination, and let's face it, courage. But to make a four hour film, to attempt to expose the reality you believe underlies the realities that everyone sees everyday, and then to be insulted by the critics and ignored by the film going public, is, to say the least of it, a blow.

To assuage the pain, to build up the bank balance, to get away from an empty home, for many reasons, Bob went on the road.

Fortunately, the crowds were still there, still eager to see Bob Dylan. He found he could still fill auditoriums from Aberdeen to Adelaide. Through the winter of '79 and on into the spring he continued to tour.

In the meantime, his plans for further film-making were shelved – Perhaps for good. It is known that he'd intended to make more films, "my next film will be about *obsession*" he's said at one point, and he told Jonathan Cott that he wanted to make at least twelve more films. However, if he would have to finance them completely by himself then film-making was out of the question.

On top of all that, Dylan had garnered some downright bitchy reviews for his 1978 release *Street Legal*. Then, when he tried to loosen up his stage presence and act a little more friendly towards his audiences – actually cracking a few jokes and telling little stories again, just like the old, old days – the Rock press came down on him and accused him of being too 'Las Vegas'. It seemed that whatever he did they were gunning for him.

The touring ended in late spring and almost immediately the strange rumors began to circulate. Strange and unpleasant rumors have been a part of the rock scene for decades. Remember the 'Paul McCartney Is Dead' rumor? But now it was being said that Bob Dylan, of all people, had been "born again" as a Christian. That he had been saved by Jesus Christ!

Consternation rippled through the Dylan legions in the wake of the rumors. If Bob Dylan – he who'd crystallized the contempt for organized religion felt by so many in the sixties with the crisp lines....

> Disillusioned words like bullets bark
> As human gods aim for their mark
> Make everything from toy guns that spark
> To flesh-colored Christs that glow in the dark
> It's easy to see without looking too far

144

That not much
Is really sacred. *It's Alright Ma (I'm Only Bleeding)*.

If that Bob Dylan had succumbed to Christianity, then what hope was there for the brave ideals of the sixties? And by implication, what did this say about everyone else?

In July 1979, the live double album recorded in Tokyo was released worldwide. *Bob Dylan Live At Budokan* did not exactly stir the critics and was widely dismissed as "more unconvincing live Bob Dylan, if you already got *Before The Flood* then you know how this will sound".

In August, an entirely new Bob Dylan was unveiled and once again, Bob confounded the world and the critics. The new album was called *Slow Train Coming* and on the cover there were definite signals of what lay within. On the front, a train rolled towards you and a pick axe handle raised high, formed a cross. On the back, a ship's mast formed another cross. The songs were once again recorded quickly but this time with a professional group of musicians and the message carried home. It was true, the incredible rumors were confirmed: Bob Dylan had indeed converted to born again Christianity.

The songs on *Slow Train Coming* had a preachy feel. Dylan sounded angry again, but this time he was angry with his own audience. Of course his audience is not a particularly religious one, and thus songs like *When You Gonna Wake Up* and *Gotta Serve Somebody* brought an unexpected message to his fans. In this, Dylan was assuming once more his old rebel stance, but this time he was rebelling against his non-believing audience.

*Slow Train Coming* was recorded in Muscle Shoals and had Mark Knopfler from the British group Dire Straits playing lovely guitar lines on several tracks. The production by Jerry Wexler and Barry Beckett was excellent. *Gotta Serve Somebody* backed by *Trouble In Mind* was released as a single, but in 1979's pop charts a hit single by Bob Dylan would be almost as miraculously strange as Bob Dylan's conversion to fundamentalist Christianity itself. It aroused little interest.

The album however sold well and reached No. 3 on the US charts. *Gotta Serve Somebody* and *Trouble In Mind* are perhaps the tracks with the clearest indications of what drove Dylan to take the step of converting to this form of religion.

To Dylan it had come down to a simple test: you either worked for the Lord or you did evil for Satan. This simplicity no doubt helped him banish the terrors and demons that had afflicted him, following his divorce and the failure of his film. In *Trouble In Mind*, Dylan exposed the roots of his pain, the

145

urge that drove him to seek salvation. In *Precious Angel*, Dylan used strong language to convey the age-old Christian fear of hellfire: "Can they imagine the darkness that will fall from on high/ When men will beg God to kill them and they won't be able to die?"

Elsewhere, there were hints that a woman had been instrumental in his conversion: "I had a woman down in Alabama, she said, "quit your messing, straighten out; you could die down here, be just another accident statistic."

Finally, there were disturbing signs that the notorious, simple-minded conservatism of fundamentalist Christianity had taken hold of Bob Dylan too. In *Slow Train* he sang about 'Sheiks walking around like kings, wearing fancy jewels and nose rings," and "All that foreign oil controlling American soil". Then in *When You Gonna Wake Up* he lamented, "Adulterers in churches, pornography in the schools..."

The last track on the album was *When He Returns*, with some very fine piano playing from Barry Beckett to accompany Dylan as he sings a heartfelt affirmation of his new faith.

As they'd done before, Dylan's fans went out and bought his new album despite the critical lambasting it received in the Rock press. However, this was no *Self Portrait*, an obvious artistic mistake, this was a completely new direction and one that was most unwelcome to many old Dylan fans.

However, Bob was determined, and on October 14 he showed up for a surprise TV appearance on Saturday Night Live. He did *Gotta Serve Somebody* first, a bit stiff and sung without much fire or convction, then returned later to get in a moving performance of *I Believe In You* and finished it all off with a rocking *When You Gonna Wake Up?* His new group included a trio of black gospel singers, Monalisa Young, Regina Havis and Helena Springs. On bass he had Tim Drummond, on guitar Fred Tackett and on drums Jim Keltner. On his TV performance Terry Young played organ, but for the live performances that were scheduled for November and beyond, Bob had lined up Spooner Oldham.

On November 1, Dylan did the first of fourteen sold out shows at San Francisco's Warfield Theatre. He performed the songs from *Slow Train Coming* and several new songs that were later to be used for his second 'Christian' album, *Saved*.

Despite calls from the audience for older songs, Bob did not perform a single song written before his conversion. In one show he said: "All old things are passed away" when the crowd cried out for *Like A Rolling Stone*.

The shows at the Warfield were produced by Bill Graham, and the theatre, a modest two thousand-seater, was far more intimate a venue than the huge auditoriums, hockey rinks and stadia that Dylan had played so often in the seventies.

To warm the crowd up the three gospel singers, accompanied by Terry Young on organ, worked their way through six numbers including a gospel tinged version of *This Train*, the old Woody Guthrie tune.

Then Dylan and the Band, Keltner, Drummond, Oldham, Tackett, came out to join in and started things off with *Gotta Serve Somebody* and follow on with the rest of the songs from *Slow Train Coming*. After an interlude, Dylan would reappear and continue with *Gonna Change My Way Of Thinking*, *Do Right To Me Baby* and then the newer songs which he'd written since recording *Slow Train Coming*, like *Covenant Woman*, *Hanging On To A Solid Rock*, *I've Been Saved (by the Blood Of The Lamb)*. For encores he would sing *Blessed Be The Name Of The Lord Forever* and *Pressing On*. In all, Bob sang seventeen songs, all of them concerning Jesus Christ and salvation and his joy at being saved.

The critical response to Dylan's "born again" music and the Winterland shows was overwhelmingly negative. Bob had expected it, he'd been through this movie before, but in 1979 Bob Dylan was less important to Rock than he had been in 1966 or at Newport in '65. The critics attacked him, dismissed his show, and many fans felt the same, but there wasn't a great surge of anti-Dylan feeling. The record continued to sell very well, surpassing *Street Legal* after just a few months.

Once more Dylan headed out on tour, taking his evangelical message with him, and still the crowds came out for him. Possibly his fans were just curious to see what this latest switch from Dylan was all about, but there was also a new element drawn to his shows, other "born again" Christians turned out in considerable numbers. Just as Dylan folk had identified each other in the sixties by wearing psychedelically patterned shirts, so now the new Christian Dylan fans wore crosses prominently displayed for all to see.

Dylan toured on into 1980 and then took several months off to prepare for his next album. He had most of the songs already written, songs like *Covenant Woman* and *Hanging On To A Solid Rock* but now he also penned *A Satisfied Mind* and *Are You Ready*.

Once more, he returned to Muscle Shoals and recorded with Jerry Wexler and Barry Beckett producing and with the same musicians that had been touring with him. The new album, *Saved*, was released by Columbia on September 9, 1980, and a single was put out at the same time with *Saved* backed by *Are You Ready*.

On *Saved*, Dylan sounded more relaxed about his new found faith. There were less preachy sounding songs, less "finger pointing", and the music was very fine too. However, Dylan, continuing to make born again Christian records, was a far less interesting item to the rock world in general than Dylan converting to this outlandish way of thinking. Hence *Saved* was reviewed here and there, not favorably, and sold disappointingly, only reaching No. 24 in the US chart.

Of course, there had always been a streak of religiosity in Bob Dylan's music and many references to Jesus Christ. After all, a song like *Lay Down Your Weary Tune* sounded almost like a hymn, and the early Dylan's fierce urge to exposure of the wicked and the corrupt was balanced by a sense of religious grace. As the young Dylan was exposed to more sophisticated philosophical forms from Zen Buddhism to the poetry of Rimbaud, so his songwriting shifted to the interior planes and focused on the constant problems of communication between human beings and the cracks of doom and "simple twists of fate" that can seperate us. Now middle-aged, and with many new and diverse pressures upon him, Bob Dylan had found, as so many artists have done, a fuller comfort, a sense of peace, in the salvation of faith in Jesus Christ.

However, to the rock scene Dylan now seemed more and more like an eccentric oddity, a figure from the distant past, almost an irrelevancy.

He continued to do short tours, covering many smaller cities across the USA through late 1980 and early '81. In the summer of '81 he recorded once again, this time with Chuck Plotkin producing. As before, he had Keltner, Drummond, and Fred Tackett playing and in addition some studio musicians, including Ronnie Wood playing guitar on one track *Heart Of Mine*. Also involved were Ringo Starr and Donald 'Duck' Dunn.

The album that resulted was called *Shot Of Love* and was released in September '81. In the songs like *Watered Down Love* and *Dead Man Dead Man* or *Property Of Jesus*, Dylan seemed determined to ram home the point that he had been saved, that he had found Jesus – and that the rest of us hadn't and therefore we're going to hell. The preachiness was back, reinforced now by a sullen sort of anger at the world. *Heart Of Mine*, backed by *The Groom's Still Waiting At The Altar*, was released as a single to coincide with the album. The album reached No. 14 in the US charts despite receiving poor reviews. One track on *Shot Of*

*Love* however was outstanding. Entitled *Every Grain Of Sand*, it provided the listener with a much more sympathetic view of Dylan's reasons for conversion without the *Me And You* anger, present in so much of his born-again music. With a slow, stately backing, *Every Grain Of Sand* shows off Dylan's own harmonica style in a very moving way, and for once the song lyrics are lovely.

> In the time of my confession
> In the hour of my deepest need
> When the pool of tears beneath my feet
> Flood every newborn seed
> There's a dying voice within me
> Reaching out somewhere...

and:

> I gaze into the doorway
> Of temptation's angry flame
> And every time I pass that way
> I always hear my name
> I hear the aging footsteps
> Like the motion of the sea
> Sometimes I turn there's someone there
> Other times its only me
> I am hanging in the balance
> Of the reality of man
> Like every sparrow failing
> Like every grain of sand.

In the middle of November 1981, Dylan set out on another tour, concentrating on smaller cities and covering the southern states of the USA very thoroughly. When that tour ended he withdrew from public view once again and very little has been heard from him since.

An occasional sighting was reported however, in particular Rolling Stone Magazine noted in summer '82 that Dylan had been seen with his eldest son, Jesse, attending a Clash concert, which seemed at the time a sign of hope.

Then from out of the blue in January 1983, Dylan announced that he intended to record again, that he was going to concentrate on songs with a "political content" and without the Christian message that had so dominated his last three albums, and that he was trying to get David Bowie to handle the production!

Once again Bob Dylan had proved himself a master of surprises.

## Chapter Twelve

# Infidels

*Infidels* – the unfaithful, the unbelievers, a word used through the centuries for enemies, for those doomed to the Inquisition, to death at the stake, or even upon a Cross...

Dylan wrote the songs for *Infidels* between the summer of '82 and the spring of '83. Coincidentally, the Israeli Army spent part of that time invading Lebanon, routing the PLO and besieging Beirut. Not long afterward there occurred the infamous massacres of Palestinians in the refugee camps in South Beirut. A Jewish army at the gates of an Arab city, a slaughter of Moslems by Christians. Hey what century is this anyway?

No surprise then to find the album exhibits a strong pro-Israel song and a general inclination to view things from a long, almost biblical perspective. *Sundown On The Union* virtually says farewell to the United States and its ideals. Brothers and sisters, we are a very long way down the road from *Blowin' In The Wind*.

By the time Dylan was ready to go into the recording studio in the spring of 1983, the focus of the rumors had changed. David Bowie was forgotten, now it was said that Robbie Shakespeare and Sly Dunbar, the reggae dubmasters of JA, were going to turn out a reggae-rocker's style Dylan album.

Dylan had said it would not be a "religious" album intrinsically, but why the use of reggae musicians? Was Bob going to sing through a blizzard of sound effects and mountainous reggae riddims?

Needless to say Dylan fandom was quite agog by mid-April when Bob went into the Power Station in New York with Robbie and Sly on bass and drums and Mark Knopfler handling production and playing guitar. Knopfler brought in Alan Clark, the keyboards man for Dire Straits, and Mick Taylor came in to lay down some lovely guitar tracks.

The rumors now had it that Bob had given up fundamentalist Christianity and was becoming a Hasidic Jew. That he was even thinking of emigrating to Israel.

Why did Bob ask for Robbie and Sly? Because he had been

much impressed with Black Uhuru's albums which the dynamic JA duo both play on and produce. Dylan was looking for a style that had vigor and fervour, he was primed with a message once again.

In another switch for Dylan, they spent considerable time in the recording studio. Even after they'd finished the actual recording they continued to work on production details until July 6 when it finally went to be mastered for pressing.

The album was released in the fall and received very mixed reviews. Generally speaking, reviewers were impressed with the music, and the careful attention to detail which makes this one of Dylan's best ever records purely on the level of sound. The Detroit blues bar boom of *Shot Of Love*, the odd chaos of *Blood On The Tracks*, not a trace of such stuff here. Where there's an echo, as on *Sundown On The Union*, it's there because Dylan wants us to hear every syllable; he has a big message for the world.

Unfortunately it's a message that sounds harsh to old Dylan fans, the reviewers for New York's Village Voice denounced Dylan for growing into a right wing, anti-Arab, pro-Israel, middle-aged American Jew. Elsewhere media reviews were kinder, finding a vigor in the music that they'd missed in the three "Christian Era" albums.

Certainly songs like *Sundown On The Union* with its lines like:
> Democracy don't rule this world, you'd better get that in your head.
> This world is ruled by violence, but I guess that's better left unsaid...

are painful to Dylan fans from the old days who remain left-leaning, politically liberal and committed to things like American democratic ideals.

Nor is there a complete absence of Dylan's Christian beliefs. He may have swung towards his Jewish heritage and Judaism itself, but *Man Of Peace* is another sermon concerning Satan and his insidious, sweet ways that could easily have fitted into *Saved* or *Slow Train Coming*.

There are songs concerning women too, from the wiser, older-sounding Dylan of *Don't Fall Apart On Me Tonight*, to the old-fashioned guy we hear lamenting in *Sweetheart Like You*. Obviously, Bob's not out to win any new feminist fans, although on this side of the Christian divide in his long career he seems a man with a wiser heart and a kinder eye.

The standout track is *I And I*, which is a great Dylan performance, simmering with heat and energy. Dylan really

151

feels this song and delivers it from somewhere deep inside. Sly and Robbie dub up as much reggae style effect as allowed and the result is superb. The question for cultist collectors must be, what kind of roots 12"ers do Sly and Robbie have up their sleeves following *Infidels*, and will they ever release something like that?

Indeed, although Robbie and Sly's roots come through, this is not the sound effect, dub monster that some Dylan fans had feared, in fact it's really very tasteful, probably the duo's neatest work in a form outside their natural dub zone.

*Infidels* was released to strong initial sales but in a year filled with such new stylists as Michael Jackson, Boy George and the Eurythmics, Dylan didn't stand out as he used to. Dylan's main fans are now, like him, getting on into middle age and are less connected with the modern day charts. *Infidels* did however reach the five hundred thousand mark in the first week of January 1984 and received a Gold Record.

Bob Dylan has many audiences now, his work spans almost a quarter of a century, but there are gulfs now between us all – the optimism of the 1960s is a forgotten mood in these more anxious, economically troubled times. For Dylan it's *Sundown On The Union*, because there are a great many Infidels now.

# DISCOGRAPHY

**BOB DYLAN SINGLES**

| US label/number | UK label/number | | |
|---|---|---|---|
| Columbia 42656 | – | Mixed Up Confusion/Corrine, Corrina | 1962 |
| – | CBS 201751 | The Times They Are A-Changin'/Honey Just Allow Me One More Chance | 1965 |
| Columbia 43242 | CBS 210753 | Subterranean Homesick Blues/She Belongs To Me | 1965 |
| – | CBS 210781 | Maggie's Farm/On The Road Again | 1965 |
| Columbia 43346 | CBS 201811 | Like A Rolling Stone/Gates Of Eden | 1965 |
| Columbia 43389 | CBS 201824 | Positively 4th Street/From A Buick Six | 1965 |
| Columbia 43477 | CBS201900 | Can You Please Crawl Out Your Window/Highway 61 Revisited | 1966 |
| – | CBS 202053 | (Sooner Or Later) One Of Us Must Know/Queen Jane Approximately | 1966 |
| Columbia 43592 | CBS202307 | Rainy Day Women Nos. 12 & 35/Pledging My Time | 1966 |
| Columbia 43683 | CBS 202258 | I Want You/Just Like Tom Thumb's Blues | 1966 |
| Columbia 44069 | CBS 2700 | Leopard-Skin Pillbox Hat/Most Likely You'll Go Your Way And I'll Go Mine | 1967 |
| Columbia 44826 | CBS4219 | I Threw It All Away/The Drifter's Escape | 1969 |
| Columbia 44926 | CBS4434 | Lay Lady Lay/Peggy Day | 1969 |
| Columbia 45004 | CBS4611 | Tonight I'll Be Staying Here With You/Country Pie | 1969 |
| Columbia 45199 | CBS 5122 | Wigwam/Copper Kettle (The Pale Moonlight) | 1970 |
| – | CBS 7092 | If Not For You/New Morning | 1971 |
| Columbia 45409 | CBS7329 | Watching The River Flow/Spanish Is The Loving Tongue | 1971 |
| Columbia 45516 | CBS 7688 | George Jackson (acoustic)/George Jackson (band) | 1971 |
| – | CBS 1158 | Just Like A Woman/I Want You (REISSUE) | 1973 |
| Columbia 45913 | CBS 1762 | Knockin' On Heaven's Door/Turkey Chase | 1973 |
| Columbia 45982 | CBS 2006 | A Fool Such As I/Lily Of The West | 1974 |
| Asylum 11033 | Island WIP 6168 | On A Night Like This/Forever Young | 1974 |
| Asylum 11043 | – | Most Likely You Go Your Way (And I'll Go Mine)/Something There Is About You | 1974 |

| | | | |
|---|---|---|---|
| Columbia 10105 | CBS 3160 | Tangled Up In Blue/If You See Her, Say Hello | 1975 |
| – | CBS 3665 | Million Dollar Bash/Tears Of Rage | 1975 |
| Columbia 10245 | CBS 3878 | Hurricane (Part 1)/Hurricane (full version) | 1976 |
| – | CBS 3945 | Lay Lady Lay/I Threw It All Away (REISSUE) | 1973 |
| Columbia 10298 | CBS 4113 | Mozambique/Oh Sister | 1976 |
| – | CBS 4859 | Rita May/Stuck Inside Of Mobile With The Memphis Blues Again | 1977 |
| Columbia | CBS 6499 | Baby Stop Crying/New Pony | 1978 |
| – | CBS 126499 | Baby Stop Crying/New Pony (12") | 1978 |
| – | CBS 6718 | Is Your Love In Vain/We Better Talk This Over | 1978 |
| – | CBS 126718 | Is Your Love In Vain/We Better Talk This Over (12") | 1978 |
| – | CBS 6935 | Changing Of The Guards/Señor | 1978 |
| – | CBS 7071 | Lay Lady Lay/I Threw It All Away (REISSUE) | 1979 |
| – | CBS 7473 | Forever Young/All Along The Watchtower/I Want You | 1979 |
| – | CBS 7828 | Precious Angel/Trouble In Mind | 1979 |
| Columbia 11072 | CBS 8134 | Gotta Serve Somebody/Gonna Change My Way Of Thinkin' | 1979 |
| – | CBS 7970 | Man Gave Names To All The Animals/When He Returns | 1979 |
| – | CBS 8743 | Saved/Are You Ready | 1980 |
| Columbia 11235 | – | Slow Train/Saved | 1980 |
| – | CBS A 1406 | Heart Of Mine/Let It Be Me | 1981 |
| – | CBS A 1460 | Lenny Bruce/Dead Man, Dead Man | 1981 |
| – | CBS A 3916 | Union Sundown/I And I | 1983 |
| – | CBS A 4055 | Jokerman/Licence To Kill | 1983 |
| Columbia 04301 | – | Sweetheart Like You/ | 1983 |

## BOB DYLAN EPs *(UK only)*

**CBS EP 6051**    DYLAN
Don't Think Twice, It's Alright/Blowin' In The Wind/Corrine, Corrina/When The Ship Comes In

**CBS EP 6064**    IF YOU GOTTA GO, GO NOW (withdrawn after being scheduled for release)
If You Gotta Go, Go Now/Mr Tambourine Man/With God On Our Side

**CBS EP 6070**    ONE TOO MANY MORNINGS
Spanish Harlem Incident/One Too Many Mornings/Oxford Town/It Ain't Me, Babe/She Belongs To Me

**CBS EP 6078**    MR TAMBOURINE MAN
Mr Tambourine Man/Subterranean Homesick Blues/It's All Over Now, Baby Blue

## BOB DYLAN ALBUMS

Columbia 8579 (US)/ CBS 62022 (UK)  BOB DYLAN                                    1962
She's No Good/Talkin' New York/In My Time Of Dyin'/Man Of Constant
Sorrow/Fixin' To Die Blues/Pretty Peggy-O/Highway 51 Blues/Gospel Plow/Baby,
Let Me Follow You Down/House Of The Risin' Sun/Freight Train Blues/Song To
Woody/See That My Grave Is Kept Clean

Columbia 8786 (US)/CBS 62193 (UK)  THE FREEWHEELIN' BOB DYLAN        1963
Blowin' In The Wind/Girl From The North Country/Masters Of War/Down The
Highway/Bob Dylan's Blues/A Hard Rain's Gonna Fall/Don't Think Twice, It's
Alright/Bob Dylan's Dream/Oxford Town/Talking World War III Blues/Corrine,
Corrina/Honey, Just Allow Me One More Chance/I Shall Be Free

Columbia 8905 (US)/CBS 62251 (UK)  THE TIMES THEY ARE A-CHANGIN'     1963
The Times They Are A-Changin'/Ballad Of Hollis Brown/With God On Our
Side/One Too Many Mornings/North Country Blues/Only A Pawn In Their
Game/Boots Of Spanish Leather/When The Ship Comes In/The Lonesome Death Of
Hattie Carroll/Restless Farewell

Columbia 8993 (US)/CBS 62429 (UK)  ANOTHER SIDE OF BOB DYLAN         1964
All I Really Want To Do/Black Crow Blues/Spanish Harlem Incident/Chimes Of
Freedom/I Shall Be Free No.10/To Ramona/Motorpsycho Nightmare/My Back
Pages/I Don't Believe You/Ballad In Plain D/It Ain't Me, Babe

Vanguard 79144 (US)/Fontana TFL 6038 (UK)  NEWPORT BROADSIDE         1964
With God On Our Side (with Joan Baez)/Ye Playboys And Playgirls (with Pete
Seeger)/other tracks by other artists

Vanguard 79148 (US)/Fontana TFL 6041 (UK)  NEWPORT EVENING CONCERT,
VOL.1                                                                1964
Blowin' In The Wind/other tracks by other artists

Columbia 9128 (US)CBS 62515 (UK)  BRINGIN' IT ALL BACK HOME          1965
Subterranean Homesick Blues/She Belongs To Me/Maggie's Farm/Love Minus Zero
– No Limit/Outlaw Blues/On The Road Again/Bob Dylan's 115th Dream/Mr
Tambourine Man/Gates Of Eden/It's Alright, Ma (I'm Only Bleeding)/It's All Over
Now, Baby Blue

Columbia 9189 (US)/CBS 62572 (UK)  HIGHWAY 61 REVISITED              1965
Like A Rolling Stone/Tombstone Blues/It Takes A Lot To Laugh, It Takes A Train To
Cry/From A Buick 6/Ballad Of A Thin Man/Queen Jane Approximately/Highway 61
Revisited/Just Like Tom Thumb's Blues/Desolation Row

Columbia 2-841 (US)/CBS 66012 (UK)  BLONDE ON BLONDE                 1966
Rainy Day Women, Nos 12 And 35/Pledging My Time/Visions Of Johanna/(Sooner
Or Later) One Of Us Must Know/I Want You/Stuck Inside Of Mobile With The
Memphis Blues Again/Leopard-Skin Pill-Box Hat/Just Like A Woman/Most Likely
You'll Go Your Way And I'll Go Mine/Temporary Like Achilles/Absolutely Sweet
Marie/4th Time Round/Obviously Five Believers/Sad-Eyed Lady Of The Lowlands

CBS 62847 (UK)  BOB DYLAN'S GREATEST HITS                            1966
Blowin' In The Wind/It Ain't Me, Babe/The Times They Are A-Changin'/Mr
Tambourine Man/It's All Over Now, Baby Blue/Subterranean Homesick Blues/
(Sooner Or Later) One Of Us Must Know/Like A Rolling Stone/Just Like A Woman/
Rainy Day Women Nos 12 And 35/I Want You

Columbia 9463 (US)  BOB DYLAN – GREATEST HITS                        1967
Rainy Day Women, Nos 12 And 35/Blowin' In The Wind/The Times Thay Are
A-Changin'/It Ain't Me, Babe/Like A Rolling Stone/Mr Tambourine Man/
Subterranean Homesick Blues/I Want You/Positively 4th Street/Just Like A Woman

(Note that the British and American 'Greatest Hits' albums are different
compilations)

Columbia 9604 (US)/CBS 63252 (UK)  JOHN WESLEY HARDING          1968
John Wesley Harding/As I Went Out One Morning/I Dreamed I Saw St
Augustine/The Drifter's Escape/All Along The Watchtower/I Am A Lonesome
Hobo/The Ballad Of Frankie Lee And Judas Priest/Dear Landlord/I Pity The Poor
Immigrant/The Wicked Messenger/Down Along The Cove/I'll Be Your Baby
Tonight

Columbia 9825 (US)/CBS 63601 (UK)  NASHVILLE SKYLINE          1969
Girl From The North Country (with Johnny Cash)/Nashville Skyline Rag/To Be
Alone With You/I Threw It All Away/Peggy Day/Lay Lady Lay/One More Night/Tell
Me That It Isn't True/Country Pie/Tonight I'll Be Staying Here With You

Columbia 30050 (US)/CBS 66250 (UK)  SELF-PORTRAIT          1970
All The Tired Horses/Alberta No.1/I Forgot More Than You'll Ever Know/Days Of
'49/Early Morning Rain/In Search Of Little Sadie/Let It Be Me/Little Sadie/Woogie
Boogie/Belle Isle/Living The Blues/Like A Rolling Stone/Copper Kettle/Gotta Travel
On/Blue Moon/The Boxer/The Mighty Quinn/Take Me As I Am/Take A Message To
Mary/It Hurts Me Too/Minstrel Boy/She Belongs To Me/Wigwam/Alberta No.2

Columbia 30290 (US)/CBS 69001 (UK)  NEW MORNING          1970
If Not For You/Day Of The Locusts/Time Passes Slowly/Went To See The
Gypsy/Winterlude/If Dogs Run Free/New Morning/Sign On The Window/One
More Weekend/The Man In Me/Three Angels/Father Of Night

Columbia 31120 (US)/CBS 67239 (UK)  MORE BOB DYLAN'S GREATEST HITS 1971
Watching The River Flow/Don't Think Twice, It's Alright/Lay Lady Lay/Stuck Inside
Of Mobile With The Memphis Blues Again/I'll Be Your Baby Tonight/All I Really
Want To Do/My Back Pages/Maggie's Farm/Tonight I'll Be Staying Here With
You/Positively 4th Street/All Along The Watchtower/The Mighty Quinn (Quinn The
Eskimo)/Just Like Tom Thumb's Blues/A Hard Rain's A-Gonna Fall/If Not For
You/Tomorrow Is A Long Time/When I Paint My Masterpiece/I Shall Be Released/
You Ain't Goin' Nowhere/Down In The Flood

Apple STCX 3385 (US and UK)  THE CONCERT FOR BANGLA DESH          1972
A Hard Rain's A-Gonna Fall/It Takes A Lot To Laugh, It Takes A Train To
Cry/Blowin' In The Wind/Mr Tambourine Man/Just Like A Woman/other tracks by
other artists

Columbia 31171 (US)/CBS 64861 (UK)  A TRIBUTE TO WOODY GUTHRIE,
PART 1                                                          1972
I Ain't Got No Home/Dear Mrs Roosevelt/The Grand Coulee Dam/other tracks by
other artists

Columbia 32460 (US)/CBS 69042 (UK)  PAT GARRETT & BILLY THE
KID  (SOUNDTRACK)                                               1973
Main Title Theme (Billy)/Cantina Theme (Workin' For The Law)/Billy I/Bunkhouse
Theme/River Theme/Turkey Chase/Knockin' On Heaven's Door/Final Theme/Billy
4/Billy 7
(Several tracks are instrumental music from the film, composed by Dylan)

Columbia 32747 (US)/CBS 69049 (UK)  DYLAN          1973
Lily Of The West/Can't Help Falling In Love/Sarah Jane/The Ballad Of Ira Hayes/Mr
Bojangles/Mary Ann/Big Yellow Taxi/A Fool Such As I/Spanish Is The Loving
Tongue

Asylum 7E 1003 (US)/Island ILPS 9261 (UK)  PLANET WAVES          1974
On A Night Like This/Going Going Gone/Tough Mama/Something There Is About
You/Forever Young/Dirge/You Angel You/Never Say Goodbye/Wedding Song

Asylum AB 201 (US)/Island IDBD 1 (UK)  BEFORE THE FLOOD          1974
Most Likely You'll Go Your Way And I'll Go Mine/Lay Lady Lay/Rainy Day Women
Nos 12 And 35/Knockin' On Heaven's Door/It Ain't Me, Babe/Ballad Of A Thin
Man/ I Shall Be Released/Endless Highway/The Night They Drove Old Dixie
Down/Stage Fright/Just Like A Woman/It's Alright, Ma (I'm Only Bleeding)/The

Shape I'm In/When You Awake/The Weight/All Along The Watchtower/Highway 61 Revisited/Like A Rolling Stone/Blowin' In The Wind

Columbia 33235 (US)/CBS 69097 (UK)  BLOOD ON THE TRACKS          1975
Tangled Up In Blue/Simple Twist Of Fate/You're A Big Girl Now/Idiot Wind/You're Gonna Make Me Lonesome When You Go/Meet Me In The Morning/Lily, Rosemary And The Jack Of Hearts/If You See Her, Say Hello/Shelter From The Storm/Buckets Of Rain

Columbia 33682 (US)/CBS 88147 (UK)  THE BASEMENT TAPES          1975
Odds And Ends/Orange Juice Blues (Blues For Breakfast)/Million Dollar Bash/Yazoo Street Scandal/Goin' To Acapulco/Katie's Been Gone/You Ain't Goin' Nowhere/ Don't Ya Tell Henry/Nothing Was Delivered/Open The Door/Homer/Long Distance Operator/This Wheel's On Fire/Lo And Behold!/Bessie Smith/Clothes Line Saga/ Apple Suckling Tree/Please Mrs Henry/Tears Of Rage/Too Much Of Nothing/Yea! Heavy And A Bottle Of Bread/Ain't No More Cane/Crash On The Levee (Down In The Flood)/Ruben Remus/Tiny Montgomery

Columbia 33893 (US)/CBS 86003 (UK)  DESIRE                      1975
Hurricane/Isis/Mozambique/One More Cup Of Coffee/Oh Sister/Joey/Romance In Durango/Black Diamond Bay/Sara

Columbia 34349 (US)/CBS 86016 (UK)  HARD RAIN                  1976
Maggie's Farm/One Too Many Mornings/Stuck Inside Of Mobile With The Memphis Blues Again/Lay Lady Lay/Oh Sister/Shelter From The Storm/You're A Big Girl Now/I Threw It All Away/Idiot Wind

Warner Bros 3WS 3146 (US)/Warner Bros K 66076 (UK)  THE BAND: THE LAST WALTZ                                                           1978
Baby Let Me Follow You Down/I Don't Believe You (She Acts Like We Never Have Met)/Forever Young/Baby Let Me Follow You Down (reprise)/I Shall Be Released/ other tracks by the band and additional guest artists

Columbia 35453 (US)/CBS 86067 (UK)  STREET LEGAL               1978
Changing Of The Guards/New Pony/No Time To Think/Baby Stop Crying/Is Your Love In Vain?/Señor (Tales Of Yankee Power)/True Love Tends To Forget/We Better Talk This Over/Where Are You Tonight?

Columbia 36067 (US)/CBS 96004 (UK)  BOB DYLAN AT BUDOKAN       1979
Mr Tambourine Man/Shelter From The Storm/Love Minus Zero – No Limit/Ballad Of A Thin Man/Don't Think Twice, It's Alright/Maggie's Farm/One More Cup Of Coffee (Valley Below)/Like A Rolling Stone/I Shall Be Released/Is Your Love In Vain/Going, Going, Gone/Blowin' In The Wind/Just Like A Woman/Oh Sister/ Simple Twist Of Fate/All Along The Watchtower/I Want You/All I Really Want To Do/Knockin' On Heaven's Door/It's Alright, Ma (I'm Only Bleeding)/Forever Young/The Times They Are A-Changin'

Columbia 36120 (US)/CBS 86095 (UK)  SLOW TRAIN COMING          1979
Gotta Serve Somebody/Precious Angel/I Believe In You/Slow Train/Gonna Change My Way Of Thinking/Do Right To Me, Baby (Do Unto Others)/When You Gonna Wake Up/Man Gave Names To All The Animals/When He Returns

Columbia 36553 (US)/CBS 86113 (UK)  SAVED                      1980
A Satisfied Mind/Saved/Covenant Woman/What Can I Do For You?/Solid Rock/ Pressing On/In The Garden/Saving Grace/Are You Ready?

Columbia 37496 (US)/CBS 85178 (UK)  SHOT OF LOVE               1981
Shot Of Love/Heart Of Mine/Property Of Jesus/Lenny Bruce/Watered-Down Love/Dead Man, Dead Man/In The Summertime/Trouble/Every Grain Of Sand

Columbia 38819 (US)/CBS 25539 (UK)  INFIDELS                   1983
Jokerman/Sweetheart Like You/Neighbourhood Bully/License To Kill/Man Of Peace/Union Sundown/I And I/Don't Fall Apart On Me Tonight

# THE BEST IN ROCK 'N' ROLL READING
Bestselling rock references

## A-Z OF ROCK SINGERS
by John Tobler

The third volume in the highly acclaimed A-Z of Rock reference series, this book turns the spotlight onto the greatest singers in the first 25 years of rock 'n' roll. Over 250 singers whose distinctive styles, songs and personalities stand out as landmarks of rock history are profiled. Presented in encyclopedic form, each entry contains career background, an assessment of the singer's best work and selected discographies.

128 pages: 60 black/white photos. 8 pages of colour. Selected discographies.
ISBN: 0 86276 139 5 p/b

## A-Z OF ROCK GUITARISTS
by Chris Charlesworth

A companion in the A-Z of Rock reference series, this book brings together the techniques and styles, personalities, classic cuts and performances of over 200 of the world's greatest rock guitarists and bass players.

128 pages: 120 black/white photos. 8 pages of colour. Index and select discographies.
ISBN: 0 86276 080 1 p/b

## A-Z OF ROCK DRUMMERS
by Harry Shapiro

Part of the popular A-Z of Rock reference series, this book focuses on the over 200 drummers who have given the beat to rock 'n' roll from the sixties to the present, from the legendary Ginger Baker to Stewart Copeland of the Police.

128 pages: 120 black/white photos and 8 pages of colour. Index and select discographies.
ISBN: 0 86276 084 4 p/b

## ROCK HERITAGE: THE SIXTIES
by Chris Charlesworth

The first volume in a trilogy on the history of rock 'n' roll, this book features a 20,000-word commentary on international developments of the most tumultuous decade in pop music, portraits of the musicians, songwriters and industry personalities in the vanguard of the rock revolution, a ten-year chronology, and a comprehensive survey of the charts, concerts, festivals and songs that were the sixties.

160 pages: 70 black/white photos. 16 pages colour. Select discography.
ISBN: 0 86276 131 X p/b

## THE PERFECT COLLECTION
Edited by Tom Hibbert

The ultimate rock list book – 200 albums to have on a desert island.

96 pages: 100 black/white photos.
ISBN: 0 86276 105 0 p/b

## RARE RECORDS
by Tom Hibbert

In-depth information on little known masterpieces and the record collecting trade. A must for all collectors.

128 pages: 50 colour and black/white photos.
ISBN: 0 86276 047 X p/b

# PROTEUS ROCKS

## The Best Rock 'n' Roll Reading from Proteus

☐ **TOYAH**
An illustrated fan's eyeview
much-liked by Toyah herself.
by Gaynor Evans
UK £1.95
US $3.95

☐ **REGGAE: DEEP ROOTS MUSIC**
The definitive history of reggae.
A major TV tie-in.
by Howard Johnson and Jim
Pines
UK £5.95
US $10.95

☐ **BOOKENDS**
The first full study of Simon
and Garfunkel, their joint and
solo careers.
by Patrick Humphries
UK £5.95
US $10.95

☐ **PRETENDERS**
The first full study of this
powerful and turbulent band.
by Chris Salewicz
UK £3.95
US $7.95

☐ **LOU REED**
A definitive profile of this
almost reclusive figure.
by Diana Clapton
UK £4.95
US $9.95.

☐ **JAMES LAST**
A fully illustrated study of this
world phenomenon of
popular music.
by Howard Elson
UK £4.95
US $9.95

☐ **RARE RECORDS**
A complete illustrated guide
to wax trash and vinyl
treasures.
by Tom Hibbert
UK £4.95
US $9.95

☐ **THE PERFECT COLLECTION**
The 200 greatest albums, the
100 greatest singles selected
and discussed by leading rock
journalists.
Edited by Tom Hibbert
UK £4.95
US $9.95

☐ **EARLY ROCKERS**
All the seminal figures of rock
'n' roll:
Berry, Little Richard, Jerry Lee,
Presley et al.
by Howard Elson
UK £4.95
US $9.95

*order form overleaf*

**KATE BUSH** ☐
Complete illustrated story of
this unique artist.
by Paul Kerton
UK £3.95
US $7.95

**BLACK SABBATH** ☐
Heavy Metal Superstars.
by Chris Welch
UK £4.95
US $9.95

**A-Z OF ROCK GUITARISTS** ☐
First illustrated encyclopaedia
of guitar greats.
by Chris Charlesworth
UK £5.95
US $10.95

**A-Z OF ROCK DRUMMERS** ☐
Over 300 great drummers in
this companion to ROCK
GUITARISTS.
by Harry Shapiro
UK £5.95
US $10.95

**CHUCK BERRY** ☐
The definitive biography of
the original Mr Rock 'n' Roll.
by Krista Reese
UK £4.95
US $8.95

**A CASE OF MADNESS** ☐
A big illustrated guide for
fans of this insane band.
by Mark Williams
UK only £1.95

**TALKING HEADS** ☐
The only illustrated book
about one of the most
innovative bands of the 70s
and 80s.
by Krista Reese
UK £4.95
US $9.95

**DURAN DURAN** ☐
The best-selling illustrated
biography.
UK £1.95
US $3.95

**A TOURIST'S GUIDE TO JAPAN** ☐
Beautifully illustrated study
of Sylvian and his colleagues.
by Arthur A. Pitt.
UK £1.95
US $3.95

**ILLUSTRATED POP QUIZ** ☐
Over 400 impossible questions
for pop geniuses only.
by Dafydd Rees and Barry
Lazell
UK £2.95
US $5.95